THE IRRESISTIBLE
POWER OF
Story
Speak

Nicholas Boothman

Published by Boothman Inc.
Email: info@nicholasboothman.com
www.nicholasboothman.com
10 9 8 7 6 5 4

For StorySpeakers everywhere.

Especially Wendy, Joanna, Thomas, Sandy, Kate, Pippa, John and Lis Blackburn, Ross Harvey, Derek Sweeney, Tim Motion, Georgina Holt, José Prazeres and my dear departed friend Tomaz Branquinho de Fonseca.

You make the simplest things sound magical and memorable. You captivate and enchant with your words, your timing and your physical delivery.

You make me laugh and ponder and wonder where the time went.

CONTENTS

What is StorySpeak?

StorySpeak is calling men's perfume "aftershave," branding Albacore tuna as "Chicken of the Sea," and telling the boxing world "I'm going to float like a butterfly and sting like a bee."

Simply put, StorySpeak turns facts into feelings.

Genius Communicators throughout history know that 80% of the time people make their decisions based on their emotions even though they think they're being rational. That's why you find StorySpeak used in business, religion, education, healthcare, law, entertainment, community, parenting and family affairs to capture the emotions and arouse enthusiasm.

When you tell someone facts they might remember them and believe them or they might not. When you conjure up those same facts in their imagination, where they can see, hear, feel, and even smell and taste them they are much more likely to remember and, more importantly, believe them.

When you simply pass on information we call it fact-speak. When you capture the emotions and bring things alive in the imagination we call it StorySpeak. And it pays off. StorySpeakers earn more, out-perform, do better at school, work and home, get hired and promoted faster and get better service in person, and over the phone than fact-speakers.

Fact-speaker: "I like my job very much."

StorySpeaker: "I tap dance to work."

Fact-speaker: "I was cold."

StorySpeaker: "I tugged up my collar, pulled down my hat and pushed my hands deep into my pockets."

When Bill Gates asked Warren Buffett "How do you like your job?" Buffett replied, "I tap dance to work." Ginger Rodgers, the legendary American actress, singer and dancer answered the same question saying "women have to do the same as men but backwards and in heels." That's all StorySpeak. Images we can see, believe and remember. They make the listener/reader part of the experience.

On the day Bill Gates resigned his chairmanship of Microsoft he was asked why he didn't come up with the iPod idea. He replied, "It's kind of like surfing. There you are out in the ocean. Sometimes you're in the perfect spot for a great wave, sometime the other guy is." That's StorySpeak too.

Steve Jobs conjured "graphical interface" into "desktop" and called the computer "a bicycle for the mind" and we all know what a "mouse" is. The names Apple, PayPal and Windows are all StorySpeak.

StorySpeak is not a new way of thinking: it's just a really useful tool for turning facts into feelings.

Don't overuse it. But always be on the lookout for opportunities capture the imagination of others. After all, the ability to arouse enthusiasm in other people is the great asset any of us possesses.

Part One: Imagination rules the world

We humans are like remote sensing stations. Every day we go out into the world and have experiences through our senses.

We put these experiences into words and explain them to ourselves. *What a beautiful day. Man! Am I hungry or what?*

Then we explain them to other people. *There I was, staring across the parking lot in the blistering sun looking for somewhere to eat when I saw this flashing blue neon sign.*

The more engaging you are at explaining your experiences to other people the more they will be drawn to you and the faster success will come your way.

It doesn't matter whether you're explaining the features of a cottage you want to sell, designing concept cars, recommending the lamb chops over the chili con carne, asking someone out on a date or applying for a promotion, people must feel they can trust you, have confidence in your logic and feel a strong tug at the heart strings.

Most people can deliver on the first two of these fundamentals: delivering on all three, at the same time is the hallmark of a Genius Communicator.

Throughout this book you'll find a series of exercises.
They are optional.
Choose only those which appeal to you.

1
The future belongs to the StorySpeakers

Ask any high school student who his or her favorite teacher is and then ask why. Chances are the answer will be, "Because she makes things more interesting" or "Because he tells stories."

When educators StorySpeak they keep their students engaged and interested by transforming learning into lively experiences.

These teachers know that a great StorySpeaker must first capture the student's imagination and hold their attention and second, transport them into another world. And they know the way to keep those students in that other world is by continually increasing the tension in the story until the conclusion is reached, the lesson learned and the message delivered.

This strategy doesn't just apply to motivating school-children—it's everywhere in society.

Advertisers polish their stories, social media spreads

them, politicians bend them, religions exalt them and motivational speakers use them to capture the hearts and minds of their audiences and transport them onto new horizons

In Business...

When things get competitive it's all about the story.

Today's corporate leaders use StorySpeak to bring their company's heritage to life in the imagination. They share their stories with their customers, their staff, their new hires. They live them. Corporate leaders StorySpeak their visions and goals.

Successful entrepreneurs StorySpeak naturally. They use stories and word pictures to quickly get their ideas across in a tasty manner and make them stick. They talk about planting seeds, bearing fruit and cutting out the deadwood. In 1975, two screenwriters walked into a Hollywood producer's office and planted three words, "jaws in space," and the blockbuster movie Alien was born. Pure StorySpeak.

Sales people know their stories are as, or more, important than their products to build trust and reinforce their brand

In Healthcare...

Patients and doctors have long understood the power of telling and listening to personal accounts. Patients want to hear the stories of other patients who've gone through the same thing.

Imagination is at the heart of one of the longest-running mysteries in western medicine: the placebo effect. This is the idea that pain or illness can be relieved through "fake" medicines like sugar pills, just because the patient believes he has received a real treatment. Researchers know the placebo effect is a perfect example of the power of the imagination to engage forces beyond a patients' conscious control.

The Annals of Internal Medicine recently published a study examining the effects of storytelling on high blood pressure. In the test group, listening to personal stories helped achieve and maintain a drop in blood pressure as effectively adding more medication. "Telling and listening to stories is the way we make sense of our lives," said Dr. Thomas K. Houston, lead author of the study at the University of Massachusetts Medical School in Worcester. "That natural tendency has the potential to alter behavior and improve health."

In Retail...

More and more companies are catching on to the importance of storytelling. At Nike, several of their senior executives are called "corporate storytellers." They explain the company's history to everyone from vice presidents and sales reps to the hourly workers who run the cash registers at Nike's stores.

The most recent advertising campaign from Domino's Pizza features true stories of franchisees saying things like "I bought my first franchise with the money I saved at college." "I mortgaged my house to buy my first franchise."

Weight Watchers couples solid data with real-world stories of people making better food choices to improve the health of their customers.

John Deere shares solid data with real-world lifestyle stories of people interested in farming.

Lego shares solid data with real-world stories about

families bonding while building together.

'The Magic of Heineken' tells of the beer company's founding in Amsterdam in 1864.

In Associations…

A famous AARP TV commercial starts: "Our story began when Ethel Percy Andrus came across a retired teacher living in a chicken coop because she could afford nothing else. It inspired her to found AARP."

Online…

Successful blogs use stories to hook the attention of their readers and transport them around the world in a million ways.

TripAdvisor is filled with true stories from people enhancing their lives as a result of their services.

TED's mission statement is to spread understanding through stories.

Facebook, Linked-in and hundreds of dating sites invite people to share their stories to fill gaps in their lives.

In Fundraising…

"A great product with a great story is a winning combination."

Fundraisers weave real-world stories into their communication efforts to capture interest, elicit engagement and get the wheels turning.

Online they use the StoryBook approach, alternating photos with short, ten second blocks of text.

The YMCA just renamed its fundraisers "storytellers."

They found that turning the spotlight on their participants, staff and volunteers was not just a great way to show gratitude for their involvement, but also a great way to connect with the community at large.

In the Courtroom...

Research shows that Jurors construct stories inside their heads to provide meaning to situations they never experienced first hand. The problem with this is they use their personal emotions, values and beliefs to evaluate the credibility of defendants, witnesses and evidence. This may not benefit the lawyer or the client.

A great trial attorney will beat them to it by planting his or her favorable take on the story so vividly in the decision-maker's imaginations, they see that version as the truth.

On the Trade Show Floor...

Stories are quick and they stick. Customers like hearing them because they quickly build trust and make relationships human and personal.

Two weeks after the show people will remember you and your stories before they remember the booth or the facts and figures.

In Love...

Romance is the art of expressing sentimental love. "Romance" is also the French word for story. At its simplest, it is amorous gestures towards the one you love. At its best, it is deliberately creating wonderful memories that serve to form a foundation of specialness on which you build the loving relationship of your life. This comes from the stories you create together. Stories you tell yourself, each other, and to other people.

Romantic means "story-worthy."

2

Fame, fortune and flying first class

Here's a black and white, fact-speak description of an event that occurred several years ago:

The limo picked me up at the airport in Las Vegas and drove me to the hotel. There was lots of traffic. The limo driver wants to be a motivational speaker.

After researching fifty-six ethical, charismatic leaders and thirty-two professional speakers, I advised the driver to learn StorySpeak, become an expert with a fresh approach, and find a way to do it for love.

Now here's the same event in StorySpeak.

I t was bucketing down as the shiny black Cadillac Escalade eased out of terminal three at McCarran Airport. The driver leaned back in my direction.

"Straight to the hotel Mr. Boothman?"

I glanced up at the mirror, "Please. The Venetian." I finished texting my client to let her know I'd arrived in Las Vegas and was on the way to the conference venue.

It was a long flight and I was tired. I leaned back against the soft leather headrest and watched passengers snatch their bags and dive into the terminal out of the rain. They can't see me, just the tinted windows.

"We had flash floods in the valley over the weekend," the driver said turning up the air-conditioning a notch. "No-one hurt."

I nodded. No need to speak. These drivers sense everything.

It was a little after five on a muggy August evening as we passed the control gates and headed southeast on Paradise Road then doubled-back north on Swenson. I'd flown in from Istanbul via Paris. Spoke there two days ago to three hundred security experts from all over the world.

"You're speaking tonight?"

"Tomorrow," I said, dialing my office to let them know I'd landed okay.

Professional Speakers are paid in full in advance, that's the good news. Missing an engagement through weather and flight cancellations can be a costly catastrophe and the stuff of a speaker's nightmares. Letting down hundreds of people and handing back tens of thousands of bucks - that's the bad news. That's why I arrive a day early when I can.

"Back straightaway after?" The driver caught my eye

again.

"No. The following day." I said. "I don't do red-eyes." Then, as an exasperated indulgence, "and I appreciate a real pillow."

This was my sixth speaking engagement in Vegas this year. There are no direct flights back to Toronto after two in the afternoon. Flying via Atlanta or Dallas and arriving home at nine in the morning - not any more.

We turned onto East Tropicana and headed west. The clouds cleared, the sun came out and we hit the rush-hour. The Escalade inched ahead in silence.

The driver was an enthusiastic soul. Couldn't have been more than twenty-five, maybe thirty tops. A city creature who radiated ambition and good health. Southern accent, fit, smart, excellent posture, symmetrical smile, red-hair combed straight back with Ray-Ban Aviator sunglasses perched on top and piercing bright blue eyes.

Been waiting for me at the baggage check holding up a tablet with my name on it. Even though I travel light the driver insisted on taking my carry-on and my shoulder bag. I hung onto my shoulder bag. My laptop never leaves me when I'm on the road.

We got stuck at a red light. A middle-aged couple both dressed as Elvis danced alongside between the lanes of halted traffic. Their exaggerated black pompadour hairdos, sunglasses and pimped-out white jumpsuits made me smile and the driver scowl. They circled around the Escalade and peered in through the smoke glass window on my side then ran off unimpressed.

"That's my dream." My driver said.

I leaned forward and looked out the windshield. "You're

serious?" This was hilarious.

"Aha."

My brain ticked. "So, what are you waiting for?'

"Easy for you to say, you're already there."

"I'm a speaker not an Elvis impersonator."

The driver chuckled at my mix-up.

"I pick up speakers every day and drive them around. That's what I do – for now. Best restaurants, best hotels, work a couple of hours a week, go on TV. Great life. I want to be a motivational speaker like you.

Leaning forward suddenly felt a little too intimate. I sat back. "Well, that's good."

"Fame. Fortune. Best hotels, fly first class, sit in the back of the car instead of in the front. I want to share the stage with famous people."

"I'm glad you've got it all figured out."

We took a slow right at the MGM Grand and headed north on Las Vegas Boulevard past The Grande Canyon Experience and The Hard Rock Café towards The Strip. Many of the biggest hotels, casinos, and resorts in the world are located on the Las Vegas Strip. Each one vying with the other to fire up the imagination with promises of pleasure, thrills and extravagance - and making it one of the most popular tourist destinations on the planet.

Why should I be the one to burst the bubble. Fame and fortune maybe. Staying in swanky hotels? Yes. Because that's where most of your events take place. Flying first class? Actually, no one flies first-class much in this business anymore, unless you're really famous. For the rest of us it's coach and, on really long flights, business class. Work a couple of hours a week? That may be the time you spend on stage but preparing for those one or two hours a week involves meetings, briefings, getting to know the client, asking the right questions and often being available at all hours to chat with leaders and teams in different parts of the continent or the world.

"What do you think a speaker does when they're not in the best restaurants and the best hotels and getting on TV?" I asked.

"I'm sorry. Am I bugging you?"

The tourists were out in full force. Swarms of grannies shuffling in and out of casinos, kids with candy, big boys with beers and big girls with cocktails right there on the street. Families with fries, franks and ice cream. Lovers in shorts and sandals posing for selfies – all playing-out in silence around me.

"Would you do this job if you didn't get paid for it?" I asked ignoring the question.

"Probably not."

I was due to speak at eleven the next morning but sound-check was at eight o'clock this evening. I should be okay for time but you never know in these hotels. The Venetian is a big place. Sometimes it can take half an hour to get from your room to the convention hall.

"In more than 20 years of speaking," I said, "I've yet to come across a really great speaker who isn't absolutely passionate about his or her message. And not only passionate but curious, hungry to learn more and desperate to stay current and help people. That's what drives me to speak and that's what drives all of us. Sure we get paid well: but that's not why we do it."

We were inching forward. The Paris on the right and the Bellagio on the left. I looked at my watch: six-twenty. The lake in front of the Bellagio reflected the Tuscan-style hotel and the lavender sky behind it. Up ahead the patrons on the patio at Mon Ami Gabi restaurant, at the foot of The Eiffel Tower, sucked on their cocktails, chugged their beers and readied their selfie-sticks to capture the imminent eruption of the spectacular fountains of the Bellagio. With any luck we'd be stuck here until half-past so I'd get to see it too.

"Why do you do it then?" I was almost relieved by the question. The conversation was getting around to what I love, and I don't like leaving conversations half finished.

"I sure as heck don't do it to share the stage with famous people. I do it for love. I'm passionate about human potential. About the amazing things we can do when we set our minds to something."

"Yeah," the driver said. "I'm cool with that."

"Motivational speakers bring people together and infect them with passion. It comes from the inside." I said. "You can't fake that, not in person. Not on a stage. You can't learn how to stand and breathe and position your hands from a speaking coach and read words written for you by a speech writer."

My phone dinged. I ignored it.

"Look inside and find out what's exploding to get out and you'll have all the style and charisma and confidence you can handle."

It dinged again. "Sound check moved to 8:30. Pls cnfrm." It was my client. I confirmed. My slides, official introduction and walk-on music had been sent 3 weeks ahead of time.

Silence up front. Then, in a throwaway voice. "So, okay. Where do I begin?"

"If you want to be a motivational speaker to be rich and famous and fly first class, don't bother, you'll never get there. Do it out of love. Do it because you have to do it, and one day you might just get rich and famous."

If you want to motivate people, there are two types of speech. If you're famous or have done something incredible and have a unique story to tell, then it's fairly easy. But most of us don't have that. If not, you've got to be very good at doing something or have done a ton of research and know a lot about something. In other words – you're an expert, and businesses pay you to share your expertize with their clients or employees and hopefully entertain them as you do it.

"All business is show business," I said, "that's the rule. And that's what separates the five hundred dollars an hour speakers from the twenty thousand dollars an hour speakers. They make things exciting. Put ideas where people can see, hear, feel and remember them – up here, in their imagination. They use StorySpeak."

"Spend an hour or two watching and listening to speakers online. Google 'speaker bureaus' and 'motivational speakers.' Hey, they all started out where you are today."

"I did that already. I've watched them all. I'm pretty good at telling stories."

"StorySpeak is more than just telling stories. It's four things. One, Talking in Color to connect with people's emotions. Two, i-Kolas, to put pictures in people's heads that they can't shake lose. Three, Point-Stories, to build a brand, change attitudes and make complicated ideas easy to understand and remember and four, Stepping-Stones to share a vision, enhance business performance, pitch a product and inspire loyalty."

"Jeepers!" The driver's jaw dropped. "That makes my head spin."

"It's easier than it sounds."

Up ahead at the lights a crowd streamed across the road towards the Bellagio.

"So, do you have a unique story to tell about your life?"

The driver inhaled sharply as if I'd hit a nerve.

"Not really."

"You're not famous? You haven't conquered some mighty problem?"

"Nope."

"Don't have a rags to riches story?"

A slow shake of the head. "Definitely not."

"Pity. If you did, you'd be half way there."

"That means I'm still here. And I'll still be here next year if I don't do something about it soon."

"Hey I'm only trying to help. I don't have a unique story either. I share my Gift. And if you don't have a truly unique story you'll have to share yours."

"I don't know anything about any gift."

"Most people don't. They don't know they have a gift, or don't recognize it when it's staring them in the face. It's like a basket of gold buried inside you. It's your personal fortune: when you find it you share it with others. Sharing it is easy: finding it is complicated."

"Basket of gold? That's a bit freaky!"

"It's the thing you can do that most people can't?

Probably something you've been great at since you were a child but never really took seriously."

"Like horseback riding?"

"That's a skill not a gift."

"Flying a helicopter?"

"No. You can fly a helicopter?"

"Since I was sixteen. They say I look too young for the tourists so they put me driving pick-up in the limos."

"Pity." That knocked me for a loop. "Anyway, no."

Michael Jackson singing "Billie-Jean" exploded outside from roadside speakers.

"Oh, perfect. Michael Jackson."

Now, there's a guy with a Gift. He joined the Jackson Five as lead singer when he was five years old. He had a voice and a performance style we had never seen before. He was an epic superstar when he was only nine.

With a whoosh and a cheer from the crowds as the fountains of The Bellagio sprung into life.

Watching them and listening to Billie Jean I felt very lucky. A picture flashed through my mind. I was ten years old and standing in the corridor at school. The teacher had been trying to explain something complicated in a math class and nobody got it. I piped up with a really simple image that explained everything - and got booted out of the class. But I found my Gift. 'I make complicated concepts sound simple and interesting.'

My musings were interrupted.

"So, how do you do this story speak?"

"How'd you get to be a helicopter pilot?" I parried back. I'd hit that nerve again. "I grew up with it."

I looked around.

"Ok." I said. "Those fountains, describe them." I closed my eyes for a second and waited.

"Jets of water going up in the air." I opened my eyes. I was hoping for better.

"Oh. A garden sprinkler?"

The driver's head went back and both hands leapt off the wheel for a second.

"That's talking in black and white – it's just the facts."

"Imagine I'm blind. Describe it. Tell me what you see."

"Plumes of white spray going up into the air."

"What kind of plumes? Where are they? How high? What kind of air? Is there a spray? What color is the air? Use your senses."

"Twirling plumes of white spray leaping ninety feet into the air against the violet Vegas sky.

"What do you hear, what do you feel?"

"And music. Wait." The driver's window dropped open.

"And an endless crash as the water drops back into the lake and the spray blows sideways away from the crowd."

"You like a challenge." I said. We were half a block away from the Venetian.

"Ha!" The driver was clearly delighted. "Ain't that something."

The car pulled a slow right turn and came to rest on the Venetian Bridge. Below, gondoliers punted to and fro in a cement lake on aquamarine water between red and white candy-striped poles. Above us ornate mosaic arches in grey and pink and a life-size replica of the iconic bell tower of St Mark's Basilica in Venice.

I thought about getting out right there and walking to the lobby, after all, the limo was prepaid by the client. But I didn't want the conversation to end so abruptly.

A flotilla of buses had the lobby blocked off. They were loading up conventioneers for a night on the town. I reached into my shoulder bag and took out a copy of my book Convince Them in 90 Seconds or Less.

I edged forward and rested the book on my knee.

"It's Julia right?" I said. She'd introduced herself at the airport.

The driver turned around in her seat until she was squarely facing me. She searched my face and nodded.

I hesitated.

"I'm Nick."

"Yes. I know." She smiled. We shook hands. Her calm blue eyes and symmetrical smile couldn't hide a fleeting sense of melancholy. "I Google all my rides."

I opened the cover and on the half title page wrote "For Julia. Do it for love." then signed and dated it.

Before I knew it Julia scooted around the Escalade and nudged the doorman aside. She insisted on taking my carry-on into the lobby. Beaming now, she threw up her hands. "I want to know more."

I pressed the book into her hand. "Page 263 will get you started. Don't rush it. Should take a couple of weeks to figure it out on your own. Get a friend to help you - it's quicker."

Her face crumpled slightly but she offered me a smile. "I'm very impatient."

"Me too," I said. "Thanks for the ride."

The doorman closed in behind herding her closer to the limo. She got the message.

She paused and turned. "See you around."

I watched her drive off then strode into the crazy opulence of The Palazzo Lobby at The Venetian Hotel.

'This place is nuts,' I thought. 'Imagination gone wild. I love my job.'

Here's question for you. Did you think the driver was male right up to the end of the chapter? Most people do and it was done deliberately to demonstrate how the human imagination regularly fills in gaps when information is missing. It manufactures details and makes assumptions. Later on you'll find out how to use this to your advantage.

In the meantime here's a simple exercise to get you in the habit of adding pictures sounds and feelings when you explain your experiences to other people.

Exercise 1: Talking in Color:

Here's a serviceable, "black and white" description of an everyday event:

"We stood in line for the bus for more than 20 minutes until the bus came. I...."

Here's the same event described in Color.

"It was frustrating; standing there in silence among all those people. The rain had just stopped, and my collar was wet. I was miserable. The lights of the buildings were shining in the puddles, and the hot dog vendor behind us was ..."

This is sensory-rich language, and the imagination – yours and theirs – revels in it.

Try it for yourself. Using the above example as your guide.

Describe your last commute to work in black and white – just the facts. Take ten seconds.

On a separate sheet of paper or on your device describe it in Color. Write it out, then take ninety seconds to describe it. The simpler and more emotional those pictures, sound and feelings, the more irresistible is the effect on your audience's imagination.

3

Who doesn't love a good story?

"Imagination rules the world."
Napoleon Bonaparte – Emperor

"Imagination is more important than knowledge."
Albert Einstein - Theoretical Physicist and Genius

Stories are to the human heart what food is to the body. Advertisers polish them, social media spreads them, politicians bend them, religions exalt them, motivational speakers and raconteurs use them to capture their audience's imagination and grasp their hearts. We watch stories unfold on stage and screen, read them in books, follow them in the headlines, gossip about them in private.

We're suckers for a good story; it's in our genes—literally, because humans are naturally curious. Curiosity is a large part of how and why we learn, create and invent, and curiosity is what keeps us listening to stories and enthusiastic about the people who tell them.

Some people's stories are more interesting and amusing

than others. Some people pay psychiatrists and consultants to help them with their stories. And, as a general rule, the better you are at working with stories, the more people will want to be around you. The worse you are, the more isolated and insecure you might feel.

We are natural-born storytellers—that's in our genes, too. We learn the basics of storytelling as soon as we learn to talk. By the age of five, we use stories to wangle, cajole and get what we want. But for many people it ends there. We still tell stories, but without the structure to make much of an impact on other people. Most of us just wander around all day with our minds wide open, waiting for someone to slip us a story.

Great orators and communicators rely on their ability to feed that imagination with what it likes best; pictures, sounds, feelings, smells and tastes.

Today's corporate leaders share their stories. Customers like hearing stories because they build trust and make relationships human and personal. Individuals like telling stories because it makes them more interesting amusing and popular.

It's a proven fact that using stories to communicate our messages and ideas is the single most powerful way to connect with customers, investors and employees – and to stay connected.

StorySpeak is more than just telling stories, it has four main components:

1.   Talking in Color to create conversation that engages people, brings ideas, products and services alive and makes them real

2.   i-Kolas to create simple word pictures on the fly

that connect with other people's emotions to lead change and problem solve

3.   Point-Stories to make simple, real-world stories with a point that build a brand, change attitudes and make complicated ideas easy to understand and remember

4.   Stepping-Stones to deliver motivational speeches and presentations that share a vision, enhance business performance, pitch a product and inspire loyalty

Practicing StorySpeak to yourself is very different to doing it with an audience, be it one or one thousand people. We come up with different words and attitudes when we address others. If you saw the movie Cast Away with Tom Hanks, you'll recall he made a volleyball into a person, named it Wilson and projected a personality onto it. Wilson became his best friend and his audience. He talked to Wilson, shared his feelings with him and asked him for advice. Wilson kept him sane.

At the dog-friendly campus of American University in Washington D.C., the Kogod School of Business lets students practice their speeches and presentations in front of "Audience-dogs." Students say talking to a dog de-stresses them, makes them happy and relaxed and helps them do a better job.

You can make your own "Wilson" audience for this exercise. Use your dog or your cat, your budgie, your sneakers, a statue in the park or your kids toys. Just remember to look them in the eye from time to time and throw them a smile.

Actors and comedians have a bunch of exercises they use to polish their improvisational skills and put their imaginations on the tips of their tongues. Speaking-Freely is one of them.

Exercise 2: Speaking-Freely

Spend ninety seconds talking non-stop on each of the topics in this exercise. Feel free to pause between each. Speak for the full ninety seconds, say whatever pops into your mind, and push yourself beyond your "common sense" barrier.

- Talk about how patience feels.
- Talk about taking risks.
- Talk about your most cherished possession.
- Talk about the texture of winter.
- Talk about one of the promises you keep making to yourself.
- Talk about courage.

4

Sensory
Preferences

It is her fortieth birthday, and Ingrid has decided to treat herself to the all-inclusive holiday in Portugal that she has always longed for.

She is wandering through the neighborhood mall when she discovers a travel agency she hadn't noticed before. There she meets Sheldon, who runs the place, and she tells him of her exciting plans.

"I just feel I need to get away and pamper myself at long last!" Ingrid enthuses, smoothing out her dress over her knees. "I'm under so much pressure at work that I really need to unwind. The tension at the office is eating me alive."

Sheldon is delighted. An obvious sale — sitting right there in front of him.

"Well," he grins. "Just feast your eyes on this!" He hands her a colorful brochure plastered with the usual palm trees and bright blue skies. "Looks fantastic, eh? Check out the color of the water — brilliant turquoise! Look at these cute villas with their red-tiled roofs! And can't you just see yourself on that long white beach?"

Ingrid slides back in her chair, her heart shrinking. Somehow Portugal feels further away than ever despite her presence in an actual travel agent's office, despite the gorgeous brochure, despite Sheldon's passionate descriptions.

There's a disconnect here. Ingrid understands the world through her feelings; she is highly kinesthetic. Sheldon, like more than half the population, is visual.

Look back at what Ingrid said: She feels that she wants to pamper herself. She longs to unwind from the pressure and tension at her office.

Her words, and her gestures and intonation are a giveaway. She uses the vocabulary of a kinesthetic person — touchy-feely, physical words. What counts most to Ingrid is how things feel. She's been dropping clues since she came in.

Now, let's play it again, Sheldon.

Our friendly, neighborhood travel agent has figured out what makes her tick and what it will take to win her over since he is now aware of how her senses stack up to take in the world.

"Okay, Ingrid. I follow you. And I've got just the place for you! You're certainly right about the pressure most of us feel at work — and you're even more right on about Portugal! I've actually been at this resort. The sand is warm and soft, and, oh, the feel of those gentle waves as they break over you and around you! And the beds in these particular villas are amazingly comfortable and cool . . ."

Sheldon is no crude manipulator. He's not lying about the beauties of Portugal and the qualities of that hotel. He has simply latched onto the same channel that Ingrid has been on for the past four decades, so the touchy-feely description he puts together will be picked up by Ingrid's own antennae. "Pressure," says the travel agent. "The feel of the gentle waves." "Warm, soft sand." "Comfortable, cool beds."

Each of us has a preferred sense. Some people respond

to the world and make their decisions based mostly on how things look (Visual), others by how things sound (Auditory) and others by physical sensation or how they feel (Kinesthetic). When you can find out the sensory preference of the people in your life you will communicate at a much deeper level.

Exercise 3: Sensory language clues

To practice identifying Visual, Auditory and Kinesthetic types of people, read each phrase and fill in a V, A or K in the box to the left with the type of person who would say it.

☐   We all have differing viewpoints.
☐   Can you grasp the basics?
☐   That sounds like a great idea.
☐   Show me how you did it.
☐   I hear you loud and clear.
☐   I see what you're saying.
☐   We're up against the wall.
☐   Can you shed some light on this problem?
☐   That name rings a bell.
☐   I can't put my finger on anything concrete.
☐   Are you tuning in to what she's saying?
☐   Let's explore a little deeper.

Recognizing which senses other people rely on to experience the world and then using this information in your dealings with them—whether personal, professional or social—can have a profound effect upon how they respond to you.

In the question period at the end of one of my seminars,

a middle-aged woman in the second row asked slowly, "Do you feel that it's hard to put your finger on what a person's sensory preference is?" This delightful woman wore a big, comfortable knit coat and was twiddling her finger slowly through her hair as she spoke. I thanked her for the question and immediately asked her not to move. Obviously a very good-natured person, she froze in position. "I'm going to ask you to repeat your question in exactly the same way," I said to her. "But I want the rest of the audience to observe. Is that okay?" She nodded, paused and repeated her question, complete with hair twiddling. There was a collective smile from the other people in the audience as they understood what they had just witnessed.

Her choice of the words "feel," "hard" and "put your finger on," her easy way of speaking, her comfortable coat, her slightly full figure and her habit of playing with her hair were quite the giveaways. She had dropped enough clues to give the whole audience a strong indication as to what this woman's sensory preference might be.

You weren't there, but what sense do you think she most relies on?

You're right on if you said Kinesthetic.

In the 1970s Richard Bandler and John Grinder, the founders of Neuro-Linguistic Programming, noticed in their early work with clients that people could be roughly divided into three types, depending on how they filtered the world through their senses. They called these types Visual, Auditory and Kinesthetic.

Visual, Auditory or Kinesthetic?

Let's say three students go to a rock concert. Sheena is primarily Visual, Roxana is Auditory and Stan is Kinesthetic. When they later describe their experience to their friends, Sheena will paint word pictures to tell what the concert looked like: "Oh, wow, you should have seen it—all these people jumping about and the singer ripped his pants and his toupee flew off!" Roxana will say what the concert sounded like: "The music was incredible. The beat was deafening; everyone was yelling and singing along. You should have heard it. It was a real screamer!" Stan, who relates to feelings and touch, will describe what it felt like: "Oh man, you could just feel the energy. The place was packed. We could hardly move, and when they played 'Crazy Train' the whole place erupted."

In other words, Visuals tend to use picture words, Auditories choose sound words and Kinesthetics favor physical words.

Because we receive our information from the outside primarily in pictures, sounds and feelings, these are the three ways in which we can be inspired: by something we see externally, or internally in our mind's eye as an image or a vision; by something we hear either externally or emanating from that little voice inside; or by something we feel or touch. Usually it's a combination of these experiences that helps us interpret the outside world, but one of these three senses—sight, sound or touch—tends to dominate the other two. It's also the best way to inspire and motivate other people.

Last year I was listening to two politicians being interviewed on the radio. They were both thinking of running for the leadership of their party. When the interviewer asked them to "voice their plans," one said, quite thoughtfully, "I'm leaning heavily toward giving it a shot." The much quicker response from the other man was "Now that we have a clearer view of the future, I can see the possibilities."

The interviewer responded, "Sounds like you're both ready to announce your intentions."

What do you reckon? Can you grasp the distinction?

The interviewer, using phrases like "voice your plans" and "announce your intentions," was probably Auditory. The first aspiring leader used physical language—"lean heavily," "give it a shot"—and spoke deliberately, indicating a Kinesthetic inclination. The second hopeful candidate had "a clearer view" and could "see the possibilities," and therefore came across as pretty Visual to me.

Of course, no one is totally Visual, utterly Auditory or one-hundred percent Kinesthetic. Naturally, we are a mixture of all three. Yet, in every person, one of these systems (rather like left- or right-handedness) dominates the other two. Studies have shown that as many as 55% of all people in our culture are motivated primarily by what they see (Visual), 15% by what they hear (Auditory) and 30% by physical sensation (Kinesthetic). Just about everyone thinks they are visual.

When you are one-on-one with someone, or with a small group where everyone knows each other, knowing which sense a person relies on most to make their decisions can be a major asset. Just saying "How does this look to you" or "How do you see this working out?" or "Can you picture this" to a visual person will go a long way to connecting deeply with them. Similarly, asking a kinesthetic person how they feel about something or saying to an auditory person "How does this sound," will have a similar effect.

But what about working with groups or people you don't know? This is where StorySpeak comes in because when you StorySpeak you talk directly to all the senses, by-passing reason and logic. Visuals can picture what you are saying, Kinesthetics can feel what you're saying and the Auditories can hear it. When you StorySpeak, you address all sensory types at the same time and in the primary language of the brain: pictures, sounds, feelings and frequently smells and tastes too.

5
Talking in Color

Beffore you can start fluently Talking in Color you first need to get into the habit of Thinking in Color.

Exercise 4: Thinking in Color

Close your eyes and imagine you are at a busy airport with an hour to spare before your flight.

Using the chart below, write down all the things you can see, hear, touch, taste and smell.

SEE	HEAR	TOUCH	SMELL	TASTE

When you have made your list take ninety seconds to conversationally describe, in sharp detail, what you see, then take another ninety seconds to do the same for what you hear, then what you feel, smell and taste.

Which of the senses came most easily and which was the most difficult? Work at improving the most difficult so you can appeal to all the senses in your audiences.

Exercise 5: Talking in Color

Line–up your "Wilson audience again and:

1. Recall a holiday you really enjoyed.

Speak-Freely only about what you saw and the way it looked for thirty seconds. Next do the same thing this time for what you heard and how it sounded. Finally the same for how it felt and made you feel.

2. Imagine your dream house.

Speak-Freely about it, in Color, for ninety seconds. Include the way things look, sound and feel. You can use smell and taste too if you want.

3. Talk in Color for ninety seconds about your most cherished possession. Include all the senses.

4. List 3 things that cheer you up

a.

b.

c.

Speak-Freely about each one, in Color, for ninety seconds. Include all senses.

5. List three changes you've undergone in the last twelve months

a.

b.

c.

Speak-Freely about each one, in Color, for ninety seconds. Include all senses.

6. Speak-Freely, in Color for ninety seconds about which of the five senses could you do without and why?

7. Name 3 things you fiercely believe in

Speak-Freely about each one, in Color, for ninety seconds. Include all senses.

8. Speak-Freely, in Color for three minutes about a place you used to go to when you were a child.

Nicholas Boothman

6
i-Kola: a picture of a thought

I'm in a pickle, in a sea of troubles. It's enough to set your teeth on edge and make your hair stand on end. In the twinkling of an eye I screwed up the courage to abandon this fool's paradise on a wild goose chase into the jaws of death and without rhyme nor reason I almost ended up as dead as a doornail.

These metaphors and similes, all coined by William Shakespeare, paint word pictures and are music to the ears. In StorySpeak we group them together and call them i-Kola. i-Kola stands for "it's kind of like a…" and it's a simple tool for converting black and white speak into StorySpeak.

An i-Kola is a picture of a thought.

We use word-pictures everyday to help people understand what we mean.

- Don't put all your eggs in one basket
- He's fit as a fiddle
- It was raining cats and dogs
- You are my sunshine

- Never look a gift horse in the mouth
- She is an old flame
- He's dull as dishwater
- She's sharp as a tack

When Warren Buffett, the second richest man in the US and holder of the unofficial title "America's Greatest Storyteller" was asked, "Do you enjoy your work?" he replied with a word picture. "I tap-dance to work." That's an i-Kola. In your imagination you can see it, hear it, feel it. It appeals to all.

Telling time: 2 seconds

Here's another example of an i-Kola, this time from Kofi Anan, the former Secretary General of The United Nations:

"The planet seems to many of us, more and more like a small boat driven by a fierce gale through dark and uncharted waters, with more and more people crowded on board, hoping desperately to survive. None of us, I suggest, can afford to ignore the condition of our fellow passengers on this little boat." Telling Time: 15 seconds.

What they are using here is the same thing we all learned about at school – using metaphors and similes to create a parallel experience.

Metaphors and similes bridge the rational sides of our minds to the sensory world, they are a way of linking our internal imagination to external reality.

We use metaphors and similes all the time to explain ideas, insights and abstractions. They are kind of like canisters for ideas. They turn abstract concepts into recognizable images in your mind: they make them see-able, hear-able, touch-able, smell-able, taste-able or any combination of the above.

Any high-school teacher will tell you a metaphor is a way of comparing one thing with another without using "like" or "as", "Music is the food of love." "She's cool." A simile is almost the same thing except it uses "like" or "as" to make the comparison. "Talking to Josh is like talking to a brick wall," or "Sophie is as cool as a cucumber." We live by them, "Life is like a box of chocolate, you never know what you're going to get." We love by them, "Baby, you're breaking my heart." We even die by them, "He's at death's door."

What's in a name?

In 1914 Frank Van Camp and his son bought the California Tuna Canning Company and changed its name to the Van Camp Seafood Company. With a simple i-Kola they turned a small fish canning plant into a billion dollar business. They reframed the colorless, relatively unpopular Albacore tuna as Chicken of the Sea.

Any successful business leader will tell you they are the most powerful tool companies have at their disposal toexplain, motivate, spread the word, problem solve, sell, teach, brain-storm, convince and get a grip on personalities and relationships. i-Kola images do away with complex clutter and are easier to remember than facts and figures.

In the Warren Buffet example he said his commute <u>is kind of like tap-dancing</u>. In the Kofi Anan story the planet <u>is kind of like a</u> small boat. Once you get the hang of doing this you can drop the "kind of like" if you wish. But for the time being it's kind of like a springboard into StorySpeak.

At a recent workshop for financial planners, the participants were asked to write down the first thing that came into their heads to complete the phrase "I am kind of like a…." (Could be an eagle, a carrot, a Sherman tank – doesn't matter. The only condition is that it must be the very first thing that jumps into your head)

Next, they were asked to take two minutes to extend the comparison. Again just to jot down whatever came to mind.

The participants were surprised and pleased with the results.

One woman said, "I have no idea where this came from. I put down, I'm kind of like a Rubik's Cube." Picking up her notes she read out what she'd written. "I'm a puzzle to some people but easy to solve when you know how. I'm Colorful, and have different sides to my personality." She sat down with a contented air about her.

A man went next. "I'm kind of like an ocean," he beamed. "I'm strong and deep. I can be wild or calm. I can lift people up and take them places." He smiled and sat down.

Next another woman chimed in. "I'm kind of like a flower," she said. "What kind of flower?" I asked. "Any kind," she said. Not a good enough image, I thought. Why not? Because I couldn't visualize her flower in my mind.

I could picture the Rubik's Cube and the ocean, but her image wasn't specific enough. For an i-Kola to work, the other person has to be able to see the same picture that the speaker is visualizing. With this woman, she might be picturing a rose and I might see a sunflower.

Knowing someone is like a Rubik's cube or like an

ocean tells you volumes about them in about seven words or less.

Exercise 6: i-Kola

Write down the first thing that comes into your head to complete the three sentences below. IT MUST BE A THING (a noun: a farm, a boat, a Rubik's Cube etc..) You can't put abstract words like person, friend, doctor.

Get your pen ready. Access your Speaking-Freely Mindset. And do it now, without thinking.

I am kind of like a _____ .

Because...

My best friend is kind of like a _____ .

Because...

My boss is kind of like a _____ .

Because...

When asked to describe the financial collapse at the end of 2008 Warren Buffett said, "Wall Street has become the world's biggest nudist beach. The tide has gone out and we can see which of the players have been swimming naked." Simple. Memorable.

On the day Bill Gates resigned his chairmanship of Microsoft he was asked why he didn't come up with the iPod idea. He replied, "It's kind of like surfing. There you are out in the ocean. Sometimes you're in the perfect spot for a great wave, sometime the other guy is." Makes sense! You can see it, hear it, feel it, smell it and even taste the salt-spray in your mind.

i-Kola lets you lodge your idea in the hearts and minds of other people. Simply replace your abstract idea or concept with a "thing." Not a wishy-washy abstract thing like "a person" or "a leader" or "happiness" but a solid picture: a steam-roller, a lighthouse or a pineapple.

I met Francesca on The Early Show in New York. The show was doing a segment on acing job interviews and had recruited viewers who needed help with this skill.

In the ten months prior to the show, Francesca, an unemployed accounts receivable specialist, had sent out three hundred twenty-nine résumés and gone to seventy-four interviews without landing a single job offer.

We spoke about the way she presented herself and I asked her to complete this sentence with a noun: a thing. "I am kind of like a..." It took her a few goes but she finally came up with "I'm kind of like a Pit Bull." I asked her "how come?" She extended the i-Kola by saying "I'm watchful, loyal, and protective."

At her seventy-fifth interview, along with all the skills detailed on her extensive résumé, when asked if she had anything else to say she said, "Yes, I'm kind of like a Pit Bull. I'm watchful, loyal, and protective." She got the job. Maybe it was just luck, but maybe the offer was made because Francesca lodged an unshakable positive image in the head of the interviewer.

A client of mine directed his staff of IT engineers and salespeople to "evangelize" their new processing system at every opportunity. Trouble was, nobody could put the benefits of the new system into simple terms. Sure, given ten minutes, each of them could describe how the system worked and bombard you with jargon, but nobody—not even the president of the company—could put it into "evangelizable" language. We applied the i-Kola technique to the system, and by day's end we had agreed on this description of the software: "GX2 (not the real name) is kind of like traveling with your clients in a glass-bottom boat. You both can see what's going on in the system at the same time."

Another client, a large architecture firm, was grappling with a disconnect between the architects and the company administrators. They were having trouble collaborating because many architects viewed the administrators as a nuisance and the administrators, in turn, saw the architects as uncooperative. We applied the i-Kola technique to their dilemma and came up with the following analogy: "ArchiTech (not their real name) is kind of like an art gallery. The administration makes sure the gallery opens on time, runs smoothly, and pays its bills. The architects are the great artists that everyone comes to see."

I-Kolas

i-Kolas give people a simple, evocative entry point to a complicated concept

- It's kind of like surfing
- I tap-dance to work
- I'm kind of like a pit-bull
- It's kind of like a glass-bottom boat

Not all i-Kolas take the form of "It's kind of like a . . . "

When he was asked to explain the trade deficit, Warren Buffet said, "Our country has been behaving like a rich family with an immense farm. In order to consume 4 percent more than they produce—that's the trade deficit—we have, day by day, been both selling pieces of the farm and increasing the mortgage on what we still own."

Brilliant! He explained a complex subject in a way that a ten-year-old could understand.

i-Kolas are terrific for problem-solving, brainstorming, convincing, motivating, teaching, and getting a grip on personalities and relationships.

It should take between three and thirty seconds to deliver an i-Kola.

Let's take a look at this simple device in action. A while back I was asked to give a keynote speech for a company to help launch a new software system. I arranged a telephone briefing to get up to speed. After ten minutes, the meeting planner realized that, apart from letting everyone know a new system was coming in, he didn't really have a theme for the launch.

"All right," I said. "Let's try something. I want you to say the very first thing that comes into your head to complete the phrase I'm about to say. I don't care what it is, but it has to be the very first thing. Ready?"

"Yep."

"The new software system is kind of like a . . . ?"

There was a brief pause at the other end of the line, then, "I don't know where this came from, but the first thing I saw was a train."

"Great," I said. "Tell me about the train."

"It's been heading in the wrong direction for a long time."

"What else?"

"We've managed to stop the train and turn it around.

Now we know where the controls are and we've got the train on the right tracks." He was on a roll. "We're ready to get everyone on board and show them where to sit and then get rolling in the right direction."

"Excellent," I said. "How would you feel about using an 'All Aboard' theme at the meeting?"

It was a simple phrase but good enough to get everyone thinking the same way.

Want some inspiration? Listen to Dylan (like a rolling stone), Jagger (I'm a king bee), Paul Simon (like a bridge over troubled water). Virtually every song written is full of i-Kolas. And what about the greatest of them all? In 1964 Muhammad Ali (then Cassius Clay) turned the boxing world on its ear when he called Sonny Liston "a big ugly bear" and declared he would "float like a butterfly and sting like a bee."

Once you get the hang of it you can leave out the "is kind of like a" part out all together.

i-Kolas should take another five to ten seconds to extend. Practice using one or two i-Kolas everyday until they become second nature. Then you might just find yourself floating like a butterfly and stinging like a bee as you tap-dance your way to work.

Exercise 7: More i-Kolas

My checking account is like a bottomless pit. These flight controls are as sloppy as a raw sausage. This air conditioner sounds like someone chopping wood in a submarine.

Your turn:

I dance like a _____

My car is as _____as a _____

My boss is a _____ when he/she's angry.

The hot sun was a _____beating down on my face.

Sentence i-Kolas

Examples:

Step 1. Select a noun (a person, place, or thing). For example, a car.

Step 2. Find a different noun to compare it to. Let's use a chariot in this example.

Step 3. Use both nouns in a sentence:

"My car is a chariot at my command."

Your turn:

Step 1. Noun:

Step 2. Compare it to:

Step 3. Sentence:

7

No point. No Presentation.

I strode along the marble floors, past the majestic columns and translucent "Acqua di Cristallo" statues in the Venetian Hotel lobby. A woman in a tank-top got out of an armchair set back in an alcove twenty feet ahead of me. I headed straight over and dropped right in where she'd been. I ruffled through my bag for my itinerary and found it. I checked out my reflection in the mirror across the alcove. What a mess. It was a great vantage point. The line-ups were insane. I counted thirty six of them, all full. I'd wait a bit. I hadn't slept on the flight and a drowsy silence crept up on me. Suddenly I was transported to another grand hotel lobby a few decades earlier.

It was the "swinging sixties" and I was in the black and white marble tiled lobby of the Savoy, London's finest luxury hotel.

London led the world in music, fashion and art back then. Cream, The Stones, and The Beatles blasted from bootleg radio stations. Twiggy, the world's first supermodel, posed for Vogue on Carnaby Street in a Mary Quant outfit, while the members of Monty Python's Flying Circus paraded about as old women in overcoats and hair rollers, and James Bond suavely saved the world in his Aston Martin DB5. It was a glamorous and exciting time to be in advertising.

I was about to get my introduction to the art of making motivational presentations from my mentor Francis Xavier Muldoon. Muldoon was the managing director of Woman, the largest-circulation weekly magazine in the U.K. He had risen from nowhere to the top of an incredibly competitive business in just three years. Francis Xavier Muldoon was what you might call socially-gifted and a legendary motivator. I was his assistant. One November afternoon I followed him down a Persian-carpeted hallway to a meeting room at The Savoy.

"Two hundred seats?" Muldoon asked the bellman as we entered.

"Right, sir. Theater, no podium," the bellman answered, and Muldoon peeled off a ten-shilling note.

"Thank you, Peter."

"But Frank," I said as Peter walked away, "Don't you want me to organize more chairs?"

"Why would that be?" Muldoon replied, walking toward the stage.

"We've got two hundred and thirty-three confirmations and only two hundred chairs."

I should have known better. Muldoon didn't make mistakes.

"Nicko," he said, with a twinkle in his eye. "Most companies will book a room with five hundred seats when they have four hundred and fifty people registered for an event. Sixty don't show up and the room's half empty. If I speak to four hundred and fifty people, I'll book a room with three hundred and fifty seats, hold a few chairs in reserve, and have the place packed. Standing room only creates an atmosphere of success. A half-empty room smells of failure. Do you get my point?"

I did.

Half an hour later the room filled with advertising executives, analysts, media buyers, the sales staff from our own ad department at Woman magazine, and some of the editorial staff. I counted eighteen people standing after much jostling for position. Lots of energy. Good buzz.

Muldoon stepped onstage and waited until the room fell quiet. Then, without so much as a "Hello" or a "Welcome" or a "Thanks for coming," he held up the latest issue of the magazine.

Looking solemnly around the room, he deliberately tore off the back cover. Then he waved it aloft and declared slowly, "Anyone who would pay seven thousand five hundred pounds (the price of a house back then) for this is a raving lunatic!"

While his audience sat in stunned silence, he broke into a smile, slapped the torn-off page against the rest of the magazine, and launched into the benefits and rewards of advertising in Woman magazine, "But attach it to this, and you have the most powerful and cost-effective vehicle this country can offer you to deliver your message to four million avid and consuming women. And why is it so popular? Why do so many people read it and trust it? Because each and every issue is a must-have weekly fix of spicy celebrity news, juicy television insider gossip, and hearty real-life stories. It's the number one choice for up-to-the-minute lifestyle treats, fresh ideas on healthy family-friendly food, and spur-of-the-moment travel deals."

Time elapsed so far: thirty seconds. And Muldoon's motivational sales pitch had this roomful of people riveted. "We are less than five minutes away from Covent Garden," Muldoon continued, holding the copy of the magazine in his hand, "where freshness, variety, excellent value, expert knowledge, high standards, and . . . "

For the next two minutes he evoked wonderful images of the market, England's largest, as a foil for what he was really talking about—the magazine. He went on to describe how to take full advantage of the magazine's massive reach. Flipping carelessly through the open magazine, he said, "Four million people step inside every week not because they drifted in but because they make a conscious decision to do so. It's part of their routine."

Muldoon switched to direct comparisons. "Woman magazine is kind of like Covent Garden Market. The market, like the magazine, has sections for eating and drinking, culture, and entertainment that deliver measurable results for their business partners. It, like the magazine, has seasonal sections that continually drive new ideas and trends." He gave them circulation figures, readership profiles, and response rates, all the time linking to the parallel experience he had created in the mind of his audience—the nearby market. It wasn't overt but Muldoon knew his audience would link the magazine to all the evocative sensory images he created when they made their next advertising decisions.

After four and a half minutes he swung into his interactive close. He summarized his speech, made a call to action and used a short emotional story that he flipped into a laugh.

I was stationed by the door, ready to do my part.

"Before you take your leave today . . . " That was my cue. I opened the doors at the left side of the stage and in marched four merchants from Covent Garden pushing two handcarts. All eyes went to the carts. "We want to present you all with a token of our gratitude for attending this afternoon." The audience applauded.

The carts were piled with white cardboard boxes the size of small briefcases. On the front of each one, the cover of the latest issue of Woman with his call to action: "Do the math. Put Woman to work today." On the back was a summary of his presentation, designed to evoke the flavor of the market. On the spine were advertiser testimonials; and inside the box was an assortment of fruit, cheeses, nuts, and of course, the latest issue of Woman in a clear plastic wrap. Muldoon was smart. He knew most people in the audience would be heading directly home after he finished his presentation and they'd peruse the package during their commute.

A little later we left the Savoy, crossed the Strand, and began the five-minute stroll back to the office. It was almost five o'clock when we passed the Nag's Head Pub, a famous hangout for newspaper, magazine, and advertising types at this time of day. My boss said, "Come on. It's too late to go back to the office now. Let's celebrate."

The "Nag's" was noisy and bustling with writers, editors, advertising sales agents, artists, and the usual 24-hour crowd that accompany the print business. There was lots of laughter, clinking glasses, and boasting about the day's adventures. Muldoon shook a few hands and slapped some backs. From out of nowhere a pint of their best bitter appeared in my hand and we joined the bantering.

Muldoon nodded at an empty table over by the window. I led the way and pulled out a chair. "Okay. Feedback time." He sat down across from me, a glass of claret in his hand. "What did you notice? What did you see?" It sounded more like a song title than one of his debriefings.

"Lots." Where to begin? "You hooked them right off the top."

Hook their Attention

A "hook" is something irresistibly interesting that grabs the attention of your audience from the get-go like citing a provocative quotation, a stunning statistic, a shocking headline or ripping the back cover off your magazine. A strong hook draws your audience in and inspires them to keep listening - or reading, in the case of this book. Your hook must match the tone of your speech and support your point.

Muldoon raised his distinguished grey eyebrows and smiled.

"When you tore off the cover and said 'Anyone who'd pay seven thousand five hundred pounds for it would be a raving lunatic' they couldn't take their eyes off you. You really got their attention."

"Excellent." He sipped his claret.

"Your point was right there at the top, too: 'when you advertise in the most powerful and cost-effective vehicle this country can offer you will deliver your message to four million avid and consuming women.'"

"Well done. You remembered the golden rule: No point - No presentation. Nothing exasperates an audience more than not knowing what they are doing there. Your point must contain a cause and effect they can relate to. Do X, and this and you will get that. Don't do it, and you won't get it. The point captures reason and logic. It means your presentation makes sense. Then all you have to do is prove your point.

Call to Action

In marketing, a call to action (CTA) is an instruction to the listener/viewer designed to provoke an immediate response. No matter how creative your speech, it still boils down to this one request. A CTA uses a commanding verb like "sign up for free", "start earning today" or "get closer to your customers", "get started here", "discover a new way", "let's start working together right now", "follow the magic".

"Before you can convince an audience of anything, you have to capture their attention. Capture their attention and you can capture their interest. Once you have their interest, you can fire up their imagination. And their hearts will surely follow." He looked across at the waitress and nodded. "Capture the waitress's attention and the food will surely follow."

I ordered steak and chips. Muldoon chose something called the "Espetada." The menu said it was "a typical Portuguese dish made of chunks of beef rubbed in garlic and salt, then barbecued and served on a skewer that hangs from a hook on a stand." It was really just a fancy name for a shish kebab.

"Nicko, eighty percent of the time people have no clue why they do anything. They make their decisions based on their emotions - on what their hearts imagine they want—

even though they think they're being rational. Once you can step inside someone's imagination with your words, you can set off a reaction that creates pictures, sounds, feelings, smells, and tastes. A sensory reaction that brings things alive and makes them real."

"See that pathway leading to the subway station?" He pointed across the street. "A blind beggar used to sit there before they cleaned up this area. The old man had a sign in his lap with just two words written on it: "I'm Blind." Passersby would drop the odd bit of change into his cap from time to time but the pickings were slim. Then, on a sunny April morning, one of the junior advertising men from the office asked if he could add a few words to the man's sign. The blind man said sure; he recognized the young man's voice as someone who often dropped in a few coins and wished him luck. The adman added three words and placed the sign back in the blind man's lap. At the end of the day, the adman stopped by to see how things had been going. The blind man said he couldn't believe his ears when the coins came tumbling in. 'What did you write on my sign?' he asked. 'Not much. I just added three words,' the adman replied. 'Three words made so much difference?' Asked the blind man. 'Three words that fire up the imagination.' The adman replied. The blind beggar insisted that the young man tell him what he'd written on the sign."

Muldoon took a long, slow sip of his claret. "Right. Where's that food?"

"Well? What did it say?"

"What did what say?"

"The sign."

"Oh that. Capture your interest, did I? With my little

story."

I laughed.

The waitress arrived balancing the food. The steak and chips were drenched in gravy. The Espetadas came with mash and onions - the pub grub touch.

Muldoon opened a linen napkin and tucked one corner into his collar. "Right. Tuck in."

"The sign, Frank?"

"Oh that. It said: 'It's spring. And I'm blind.'"

"Ha! Clever. It made people stop and think—imagine what it would be like to be the beggar," I said. "And it captured a few hearts."

"Exactly. And, more to the point, it captured wallets, too." Muldoon wiped his fingers on the napkin and sipped his claret. "Solid data coupled with real-world stories is a humble and powerful potion, Nicko. It all comes down to a few catchy emotional words. They should hit four hot buttons and trigger a reward." He tapped his finger on the table as he reeled them off. "Attention. Interest. Desire. Action."

"A business presentation is kind of like this shish-kebab. It's a quick pitch with a hook, a point, some steak and some sizzle. By presentation I mean anything you do to convince others to take action." He picked up his fork. "The hook get's their attention like a television headline. There's your A." He clicked his fork against the metal hook on the kebab.

"Attention."

"The point tells them why they should be interested - what's in it for them, the onion represents your emotional set-up and the problem or opportunity." That's your I."

Click. "For interest."

"The steak," he continued, "is your solid data - the logical stuff—the facts and figures to back up your point so you make sense.

"The sizzle is the fun stuff, the real-world anecdotes - the emotional, memorable, satisfying part. Blended together steak and sizzle are a powerful and humble potion. That's D. Desire." Another click.

He leaned forward and sniffed the kebab.

"And if the whole thing looks good and smells good, then you roll up your sleeves and . . ." Click, click. "Take Action. Let's eat."

My phone buzzed and I snapped out of my daydream. I was back in the lobby of The Venetian hotel. I looked at my watch. 7:35. "Jeepers! The sound-check's in an hour." Thank goodness I'd set an alarm.

And now I was starving.

Hook Examples

Here are seven types of hook:

Hot Button Hook

- The three most common hot buttons are health, emotions, and the wallet.

- When was the last time you pampered your feet?

- Have you ever fallen in love at first sight?

- How many fund choices are too many?

The Action Hook

- I was sitting on the dock at my cottage last summer when an alligator swam out from underneath the dinghy.
- A farmer was plowing his field one morning when the horse broke loose and headed for the hills.
- We were hurtling through the back roads of Lisbon in a cab last month in the pouring rain when...

The Intrigue Hook

- Any day soon we're going to run out of options in the emergency department.
- The guys on the sixth floor think they have a secret.
- The last person he expected to see on his doorstep was his father.

The Character Hook

- After nineteen years in Seattle, Rosalie Merchant decided to go back home.
- Vladimir Melnikov was a circus strongman in Minsk before he became a financial planner in Bermuda.
- I was lucky - I found what I loved to do early in life.

The Mood Hook

- I'd checked into the hotel in Pittsburg just before noon

and headed straight for my room. Laughter was coming from rooms all around me.

- Last Sunday I sat on my porch at dawn watching the sun come up.

- As I sipped my coffee, and enjoyed the peace, security and freedom we share in this beautiful part of Canada, I couldn't help reflect how, with all the troubles going on in the world, we have so much to be grateful for. That's when I noticed an advertisement for "The Ultimate Rust Prevention" on top of a pile of papers next to me.

The Quotes Hook

- When Ann Landers said, " Don't accept your dog's admiration as conclusive evidence that you are wonderful" she…

- What did Woody Allen really mean when he said, "Eighty percent of success is showing up?" We can only …

- "If someone betrays you once," Eleanor Roosevelt said, "it's their fault; if they betray you twice, it's your fault." Today …

The Statistics Hook

About a thousand hectares of old growth forest is clear-cut on the island of Tasmania every year.

People who actively socialize are three times less likely to die of medical illness than those who don't.

Of the one hundred largest "economies" in the world, fifty-three are giant corporations. The other forty-seven are nation states.

Exercise 8: Hooks

Using the example: "Sales are down so here's what we're going to do about it," invent 7 hooks: one from each category.

- ☐ A Hot Button Hook
- ☐ An Action Hook
- ☐ An Intrigue Hook
- ☐ A Character Hook
- ☐ A Mood Hook
- ☐ A Quotes Hook
- ☐ A Statistics Hook

Nicholas Boothman

8

What's an hour of your time worth?

Check-in at The Venetian was friendly and fast. I dumped my bags in my room, freshened-up, and made it to the sound-check bang on time.

The next morning the speech was a hit. Two hundred and thirty pharmaceutical engineers and sales people. Standing ovation. Book signings and questions afterwards.

By 12:45 I'd thanked and bid farewell to my client and her staff before they moved on to the next event.

The cleanup crew moved in so I headed out the door back onto the marble-floors of The Venetian hallway. Good habits taught me to check I'd left nothing behind. I rummaged through my shoulder bag on a cruiser table by the door and took stock. All good.

A young woman carrying a small string bag and dressed in a white cotton shirt with a short blue skirt came towards me. She dropped the string bag on the cruiser table. There was no small talk.

She cleared her throat and perched her Ray-Bans on top of her slicked back red hair. "Mr. Boothman I have a proposition to put to you." She stared at me trying to gauge my reaction in advance. "I want to buy an hour of your time?" There was an echo in the hall. "What's it worth?"

I smelled a set-up. "What kind of question is that?"

"You are an expert at helping people." She reached into the string bag, took out an envelope and pushed it towards me.

"I can pay you one thousand dollars for an hour of your time." There was a look of determination in her eyes.

An elderly couple with baggy shorts, 'What happens in Vegas' T-shirts and Stilton legs gave me a dirty look.

"You're kidding, right?"

She was a different person from the enthusiastic soul who picked me up at the airport yesterday. I was surprised at her boldness. But not by her action. I'd heard of this before. A guy I know once offered the top real estate developer in his city ten thousand dollars, his entire savings and then some, if he could shadow him for one day. The developer took it. He gave it back at the end of the day along with a job offer.

"Help me find my Gift."

"That's a handsome offer Julia but I can't take your money. I have to get back to Canada."

Hesitation flickered for an instant behind the very bright blue eyes then she glanced nervously sideways at a slim gold wristwatch on a well-worn crocodile strap. Patek Philippe. Must be worth more than thirty grand.

"I don't have time, I'm afraid," I said trying to wriggle out of it. "I have a flight to catch."

"Yes tomorrow." She blushed and turned away "I don't do red-eyes. And I appreciate a real pillow." She quoted my words of yesterday in a pretty fair imitation of my English accent. She looked back a me and pointed at her temple. "And I don't forget things."

There was something curiously impressive about her willingness to go for what she wanted.

"Who do you think is driving you to the airport?" She nodded emphatically and held up her left hand to stop me from interrupting.

"I read your book from cover to cover last night." Her voice was steady and sincere. "It's up to you of course, but you said you were passionate about human potential." She rested her hand on the envelope. "Is this not enough passion for you?" She pushed the envelope further towards me. I picked it up. She didn't flinch.

I was trying to think it through, put myself in her shoes. "There are no guarantees."

"You said I must look inside and find out what's exploding to get out. Well I looked. And I know what it is. And I have enough passion for a thousand people."

Somewhere in the distance a rumble of wheels and rattling plates approached. She stared at me hard for several moments then spoke again.

"I grew up on a ranch in New Mexico. Me, my dad and three step-brothers. A year and a half ago I witnessed my father's death." The desperation had gone out of her voice and she was trying to sound more rational than emotional. "First it was a cough, then a cold, then he couldn't breathe. It was like a huge rock had fallen on me. In the course of ten months I lost my father and my home." she shrugged her shoulders.

Unable to think of anything useful to say, I put the

envelope back on the table. "I'm very sorry. But, I can't do this."

She hadn't finished. "And I lost my dignity." She arched an eyebrow and gave me a strange look. "I experienced extreme humiliation." She took hold of the table with both hands and leaned forward. She turned her head and fixed her eyes on the window but her gaze was far away. She shook off whatever she was seeing and turned back to face me.

"You can lose many things in life. But when you lose your dignity you lose you're joy and your confidence and you feel like dirt."

Her eyes swept across my face. It seemed like memory after memory was being relinquished. Her tear ducts welled-up as a wave of emotion swept over her.

"But I climbed back alone from the betrayal, the shame and the disgrace. And now I'm proud and feeling good and I'm full of joy. You can find joy when you know where to look but it's not where you think it is. That's my burning, exploding message. And I don't need paying to say it because I got my dignity back on my own." She reached across and grabbed a bunch of paper napkins from the cruiser table. "But I did some things I didn't know I was capable of. That's why I need to put my finger on my gift."

And then, looking all alone, under a crystal chandelier in the marble splendor of the Venetian Hotel she blew her nose, pulled down her Ray-Bans, put her hands on her hips and laughed out loud.

"So, whatever you say, I'll never give up. I'm not going to hold my past against myself and I'm not going to hide it. I'm going to share it." She picked up the envelope.

"Take it," she said looking straight at me. "I didn't lose everything." She raised her right arm so I could see her wrist. "My dad left his antique watch collection to me – and a couple of other things. Didn't go down too well with my step-brothers." She rubbed her right upper arm with her left hand. Something about the way she did it made me think maybe she'd taken a beating. Or more than one. "So seven months ago I packed my bags and took off for Las Vegas."

A hotel employee with a badge came over.

"Scuse me sir, madam." He searched our faces and used his body language to signal the cruiser table we were using had to go.

Julia thrust the money at me. "Take the money. Please. You're going to earn it." Who was I kidding. I got into this business because I'm passionate about human potential.

"Alright. But we need somewhere you'll feel safe. "

On the far side of the hall a line of sofas faced each other separated by low glass tables.

"Five-thirty over there."

"Uhuh." She waved my plan aside impatiently. "I'll pick you up at the front door in two hours." She consulted the Patek Philippe. "Three o'clock."

9
Business Stories

"A great product with a great story is a winning combination."

In 1762, John Montagu, the 4th Earl of Sandwich, had a good idea. He was a big-time gambler who didn't like to leave the gaming table. When he became hungry, he told his servants, "Bring me a slice of meat between two slices of bread." this was the birth of the sandwich.

Henry Heinz had a good idea: he put tomato ketchup in glass bottles. Levi Strauss had a good idea: he made trousers out of tent cloth and rivets. John Kimberly and Charles Clark had a good idea: a soft tissue paper to remove cold cream. Bill Gates had a good idea: to put a computer on every desk.

Today you can eat a cheese sandwich while you boot up Windows in your Levi's and wipe the ketchup off your fingers with a Kleenex. Because these are not only good enduring ideas, they have a great story to tell.

Businesses tell lots of different types of stories: founding stories, stories to demonstrate values, stories about growth and innovation, stories about new products and new successes, and stories to explain away upsets and calamities.

When things get competitive it's all about the story.

Solid data coupled with real-world stories make a humble and powerful potion. More and more companies are catching on to the importance of storytelling. At Nike, several of their senior executives are called "corporate storytellers." They explain the company's history to everyone from vice presidents and sales reps to the hourly workers who run the cash registers at Nike's stores. Weight Watchers couples solid data with real-world stories of people making better choices to improve the health of their customers. John Deere shares solid data with real-world lifestyle stories of people interested in farming. Lego shares solid data with real-world stories about families bonding while building together. TripAdvisor is filled with true stories from people around the world enhancing their lives as a result of the companies services. TED's mission statement is to spread understanding through stories. 'The Magic of Heineken' tells of the beer company's founding in Amsterdam in 1864. The YMCA just renamed its fundraisers "storytellers."

In StorySpeak we use stories in two ways. One, as direct experiences, where you tell a straightforward, factual story as it unfolded at the time. Two, as a parallel experience, where a story about one thing represents something else. Both types differ from run-of-the-mill conversational stories in that they must make a point. The teller must be able to answer the question, "What's the moral of the story?"

The story of Ingrid's vacation on page 29 was a parallel experience story using her search for the perfect vacation as a way of explaining sensory preferences. You'll remember an i-Kola does the same thing, it uses a mental image – "I'm kind of like a pit-bull," (page 60) to represent loyalty and persistence.

Exercise 9: Your direct experience story.

Take at least 15 minutes to jot down whatever pops to mind about your life from birth up to today in the third person, in other words, as if you're telling the story about someone else. Point form is ok. Tip: if you're having trouble getting started try beginning with "once upon a time there was a little boy/girl/baby called (your name)........" You can always dump the "once upon a time" later. You may end up with several pages. That's fine.

Next, go through your story and focus on the really important points. What mattered more, winning that Little League game at eleven, or beating out a hundred applicants for your first-ever job? Your dog dying when you were fifteen, or being dumped by your big crush in tenth grade? (Don't be afraid to admit it if the dog's death hurt more!) Keep whittling away until you can read or tell your story in ninety seconds or less (about 200 words) without your notes. You'll find by doing this that key experiences come into focus, and certain patterns may emerge. You'll have a sense of the essential "you" in a nutshell.

Finally change the story back into the first person: "I was born in Wyoming, but my family kept moving till I was twelve...". And so on.

StorySpeak makes comprehension and absorption easy because stories have recognizable patterns, and in those patterns we find shared meaning and satisfaction. It's a fancy kind of shish-kebab and the pattern looks like this:

Another example of a direct experience story might be explaining how you became so frustrated with your life you decided to take a risk and try something completely different - and that it really paid off.

A parallel experience story might use that same story to demonstrate "the only limitations we have are the ones we put on ourselves," and how, when you step out of your comfort zone, you discover the rewards of taking a risk and you want to try more new things.

Shish-Kebab

The shish-kebab is a framework. But it is flexible. Sometimes the hook and the point need to swap places to make the flow more natural. You don't always need a "call to action" and occasionally you need a few more chunks of steak and sizzle.

Hook

Point

Set-up (who, where, when)

Problem/Opportunity (what?)

Steak and Sizzle Examples

Solution (how?)

Payoff/Emotional close

Moral of the story/point/call to action

Here's a true story from one of my workshops: These are the notes on which Anshu built her story.

Hook – I was jammed into the subway at rush-hour. I was bored, I was stuck, and I was trapped by 'the golden handcuffs' at work. I wanted something different – something interesting – something that would light me up. Then I saw an ad above the doors in front of me.

Point – "The biggest risk is taking no risk at all."

Set-up - I'd steadily climbed the career ladder as a Chartered Accountant in Northern Canada for the last twenty years. I had everything. Great house, loving husband, two teenage daughters. I had an amazing job on paper - good pay, good security, prestigious, well respected

Problem - but I couldn't imagine doing it for 20 more years: but how could I possibly give it all up?

Steak and sizzle #1 - I asked myself, if I could do anything, what would I do? Where would I live? My dream job was to share with people the things I had learned about living a happier life. My dream place to live was the Mayan Riviera in the areas where people had very little, but always seemed so happy. *Describe in Color for ninety seconds and include a short anecdote.*

Steak and sizzle #2 - How would I handle my family? When I told our two teenage daughters they were shocked but gave me their half-hearted support. My husband did a deal with his boss to work two long weeks on and two off. It meant a safety net - and a lot of flying for him, three thousand miles from Grande Prairie in the frozen north of

Canada to the sunny south of Mexico every two weeks. *Describe in Color for ninety seconds and include a short anecdote.*

Steak and sizzle #3 — What was I going to do? Being a logical, practical, get-things done kind of girl I immediately started figuring out what to do.

Solution - I built a business around a light-hearted fun one hour happiness self-improvement session to be offered at resorts and wrote a book called 'Happy Hour' based on the program. The move took two years and a lot of work and planning, but we made it, all four of us. Much to the shock and surprise of everyone we knew! *Describe in Color for ninety seconds and include a short anecdote.*

Payoff/Emotional close - Risking it all – making this huge life-shift when everyone thought we were crazy has been the best thing in the world for our entire family. It has changed our lives. Changed our perspectives. Changed us forever. And…we aren't done.

Restate the point/Moral of the story - I wanted something different – something interesting – something that would light me up. I took a risk and I found it. Once you discover the effects that taking a risk has on you…you aren't scared anymore. You know the risk is worth it. It frees you. Anything you want is possible. And we knew for sure the biggest risk is taking no risk at all.

Telling time: 10 – 15 minutes

What do you think a team of engineers or realtors or entrepreneurs can learn about innovation from a jaded accountant from the frozen north?

Anshu's story is entertaining enough as a direct experience. But it also works really well when, as a corporate motivational speaker, Anshu uses it as a parallel story to illustrate "the only limitations we have are the ones we put on ourselves."

Exercise 10: Expand these notes into a leadership story.

What can a budding entrepreneur learn from The Earl of Sandwich?

Hook – "It was a cold evening in April and John Montagu's tummy had been rumbling for an hour."

Point – A leader is someone who knows what to do - and does it.

Set-up - "Let me tell you about John Montagu, the . . . .

Problem – He was a big-time gambler who didn't like to leave the gaming table even when he was hungry so he came up with an idea.

Steak and Sizzle 1, 2 and 3: "First John Montagu knew what he wanted…. Second, he looked at his options and took stock of his resources: his people, his supplies…. Third, he took action by….

Solution: The birth of the sandwich.

Moral of the story – A leader knows what to do – and does it. So, the next time…

10
The Moral of the Story

Throughout history, great speakers and writers not only entertained people, they instructed them on how to improve their lives. Their stories revolved around "morals." A moral in a story is a message or a lesson learned from the story or event. The moral can be left for the audience to figure out for themselves, or can be pointed out explicitly with a phrase like "the moral of the story is ..." or "the point of the story is..". Same goes for the call to action.

The Boy Who Cried Wolf is a fable, a made-up story to convey a moral lesson. It's about a shepherd boy who falsely cried out "Wolf, Wolf. The wolf is carrying away a lamb". Farmers working in the fields came running and asked him, "Where is the wolf?" The boy laughed and said "It was just a joke." He played the same trick again over the next few days and when a wolf really did come, he cried out but no one came. Moral of the story? Liars can't be trusted.

Fable's typically feature animals to get their message across. They are great for children but seem patronizing in business. Nevertheless, the moral of a business story is paramount - and the best place to begin creating your story.

Here's a parallel business story.

Motivation works best when you say what you want.

When was the last time you saw a horse eat a hamburger?

Mike, an airline captain, lives on a farm in a very picturesque part of the countryside just outside Omaha, Nebraska. Mike's neighbor, Anna-Lisa, raises horses. At weekends people come out from the city to enjoy the sights and sounds of nature. Sometimes, they stop and feed Anna-Lisa's horses.

"They're driving me nuts," Anna-Lisa told Mike one Saturday morning. "Horses don't eat left over hamburgers and pizza: they're vegetarians, for heavens sake! They just sniff it and drop it right there. Before long it attracts flies and rats and dogs. So, I put up a sign 'Do Not Feed The Horses,' but the problem got worse."

"I'm not surprised," Mike said. "Now people who'd never even thought about feeding the horses until they saw your sign thought 'oh let's feed the horses.'"

"I thought it was because the sign was too pushy," Anna-Lisa told him, "so I changed it to read 'Please Do Not Feed The Horses,' but it got even worse."

"No kidding? Now people think whoever put this sign up is polite. They won't mind if we feed the horses!"

"Mike, you've got to help me I'm at my wit's end."

Mike scribbled a few words on a scrap of paper. "Try putting this on your sign."

Mike didn't see Anna-Lisa again until the end of summer. One evening her truck pulled up in his driveway and Anna-Lisa got out smiling. "Mike, it worked like magic."

"Of course, because you said what you want – instead of what you don't want. Imagine if I announced to a plane full of nervous passenger 'we don't anticipate any rough weather, so we shouldn't encounter any bumps, and if everything goes according to plan, there shouldn't be any problem arriving on time in London,' when what I really mean is 'Sit back and relax, it's going to be a smooth flight, and we'll be arriving on time.'"

"When you want to motivate people to take action; tell them what you want in the positive."

That was three years ago. If you drive by Anna-Lisa's place today you can see the sign for yourself. It simply reads, "We only eat apples and carrots."

Moral of the story: Motivation works best when you say what you want.

Telling Time: 90 Seconds

The apples and carrots story never really happened like that. It's based on a sign I saw when I drove by a horse farm near where I live. It read – "We only eat apples and carrots." It's perfectly fine to base your parallel stories on day to day events and situations that inspire you. When I was looking for a way to motivate people to say what they want rather than what they don't want the apples and carrots sign popped into my head.

See if you can recognize the parts of the story:

The point – motivation works best when you say what you want

The hook - when was the last time you saw a horse eat a hamburger?

The Set-up – Mike and Anna-Lisa, one Saturday morning on a farm in a picturesque part of the countryside

The problem – garbage/language

Steak and sizzle - 3-tries resolution - 3 attempts using a sign.

The payoff – it worked like a charm

Moral of the story: motivation works best when you say what you want

Start with the point.

Complete the following three exercises. Start with the point and make sure it connects with the moral of the story. Next, add the set-up. Then introduce the Problem/Opportunity. Fill in the Steak and Sizzle examples. Finally find your Hook.

Exercise 11: a bad decision at work

In note form prepare a direct story about a time you made a bad decision at work and what you learned from it.

Hook

Point

Set-up (who, where, when)

Problem/Opportunity (what?)

Steak and Sizzle Examples

Solution (how?)

Payoff/Emotional close

Moral of the story/point/call to action

What can a team of paramedics learn from this story?

Exercise 12: a good decision at home

Prepare and tell a 90-second Point-Story about a time when you made a good decision at home and what you learned from it.

Hook

Point

Set-up (who, where, when)

Problem/Opportunity (what?)

Steak and Sizzle Examples

Solution (how?)

Payoff/Emotional close

Moral of the story/point/call to action

What can a team of HR professionals learn from this story?

Exercise 13: what I learned from a success

Prepare and tell a 90-second Point-Story about a success you've had.

Hook

Point

Set-up (who, where, when)

Problem/Opportunity (what?)

Steak and Sizzle Examples

Solution (how?)

Payoff/Emotional close

Moral of the story/point/call to action

What can a landscaping company learn from this story?

Exercise 14: The moral of the story

Here are five statements. You don't have to agree with them, just chose one and develop a 90-second story that ends up with the statement as the moral of the story.

- Cats are smarter than dogs.
- The cure for boredom is curiosity.
- Eating between meals can make you fat.
- Learn from your mistakes.
- The purpose of life is to live it.

11
StoryCrafting

L ook back on what you have learned so far about StorySpeak. Your trail of memory and imagination now embraces structure, scene-setting, shish-kebabs, Talking in Color, i-Kolas and Storytelling.

Time to bring it all together. Take your time and create a parallel story for each of the following. Remember to Talk in Color from time to time and add at least one i-Kola in each story.

A teleprompter program on your laptop might come in useful about here. You can try Teleprompter from the Mac App Store or Telekast for Windows.

Exercise 15: Parallel Story

What can a construction foreman learn about efficiency from a single mother of three?

Let me tell you a little story about …..

Exercise 16: Parallel Story

What can a realtor learn about friendliness from a hotel concierge?

Let me tell you a little story about…….

Exercise 17: Parallel Story

What can an airline learn about scheduling from a flock of geese?

Let me tell you a little story about.......

Top Ten Tests for a Story

Your stories should be tight and to the point. There is no room for digressions or distractions. Check your stories against the ten tests below and adjust them to optimize their performance.

1. Does it address the three key questions: "So what?" "Who cares?" and "What's in it for me?"

2. Does it have a point? Remember: No point? No story. What's your point?

3. Is it different (not just another office story)? Make it interesting, unusual, even triumphant.

4. Is it emotional? Does it connect with the emotions of your audience?

5. Does it both show and tell? Besides conveying a timeline of events, does your story describe how things look, sound, feel, smell, and taste? For best effect, it should convey at least some sensory information.

6. Is it short and simple?

7. Could a ten-year-old understand it?

8. Is it entertaining?

9. Does it ring true?

10. Have you avoided overly detailed descriptions of people, places, and things? Have you left out the parts that don't directly affect the story?

12
Stagecraft

You have your substance. Now it's time to add the style.

Your attitude is the first thing your audience picks up on. There are two distinct classes of attitude: useful ones that attract, and useless ones that repel. Warm, playful and patient are examples of the useful sort. Angry, impatient and cynical typify the other sort.

The good thing about attitude is you can adjust it whenever you want to be happy, enthusiastic, curious or on the top of your game. All it takes is practice. Speakers, actors, TV personalities and fashion models have trigger words or phrases to get them in the mood. They use them all the time. One might say "showtime" as they head out into the spotlight, another "Let's go get 'em," or, "Great, great, great!" and their whole being changes. They are "on" - they almost literally switch on a bright, energetic attitude. You can do the same.

Exercise 18: A Really Useful Attitude

Look at this list of Really Useful Attitudes:

Warm, Enthusiastic, Confident, Supportive, Relaxed, Obliging, Curious, Resourceful, Comfortable, Helpful, Engaging, Laid back, Patient, Welcoming, Cheery, Interested,

Courageous

... and answer the following questions:

What is the ideal me that I would like everyone to see?

What kind of attitudes can I adopt to present the best possible me?

What are some specific ways I can convey my best attitude(s) when I speak to an audience?

How am I going to trigger that attitude whenever I want it?

Dress the Part

If the first thing someone notices about you is your attitude, the second is your clothes. In fact, the impact is made so quickly it's as if they see both things at the same time and then form their first impressions about you. Your clothing speaks volumes. It tells people what kind of person you see yourself as. It also can reveal a lot about your socio-economic status, whether you're conventional or flamboyant, sexy or modest, trendy or traditional.

The iconic French designer Coco Chanel once said, "Dress poorly, and people will notice your clothes; dress well, and people will notice you." Ask yourself: What do I want my clothing to communicate to others? Is there an aspect of my personality that I want to emphasize? Does my current wardrobe do the job? Take into account your physical characteristics and make sure the image you want to create works with them.

The way we dress influences our behavior and attitude, and that in turn influences the attitudes of other people. As with other forms of packaging, is the better you dress, the more seriously people will treat you.

Assume The Best

Generalizations so often lead to dangerous, limiting, biased, unfair assumptions. Assumptions at their worst are nothing more than convenient fantasies. At their best, though, assumptions are a terrific learning tool.

Assume rapport and trust between yourself and your audience.

Assume/trust that you (will) like them and that they (will) like you.

Assume that what you do with other people — speaking, relating, empowering, etc. — will work.

Assume the audience is very forgiving – because most of them are.

Assume Rapport

Assuming rapport is how socially-gifted people make most of their initial connections. They simply turn up next to, in front of, on the other end of the line from, the person they want to connect with and carry on as if they've already know them for years.

Think of your local priest, rabbi, mullah or other religious leader, ninety-nine percent of the time they just assume they know you and get on with the business at hand. It's one of the skills you learn as you get older and more seasoned at connecting with other people: but there's no reason you can't assume rapport at any age. As infants we are great at assuming rapport. But then somewhere between toddlerhood and childhood we somehow manage to become intimidated by others for a few decades. Then, thirty or forty years later the lucky ones revert back to the open, friendly innocence of childhood.

The idea behind assuming rapport is that you don't use any

particular opening line – you just start talking. The more you learn to include the ongoing reality the more easy and natural you will appear.

Exercise 19: Assuming Rapport

Strike up four conversations in the next 24 hours with perfect strangers of the opposite sex and of any age, using Occasion/Location statements or questions.

Be Congruent

When your body language, your facial expressions, your voice tone and your words are all saying the same thing, people will believe and trust you.

Make Eye Contact

Eye contact says "trust is in the air." Be sure not to overdo it.

Find Common Ground

At the heart of the process of establishing instant rapport is the hunt for common ground. The quicker you can find things in common with the audience, the faster rapport will be established.

You know the feeling of satisfaction you get when someone really understands you, when you spill your guts about something that's dear to your heart and your listener says empathetically, "I feel that way too"? That kind of empathy is one of the most powerful triggers you have to connect with your audience and cement the sense that you're sharing common ground.

A Great, Great, Great Smile

The quickest way to put your best face forward is with a smile. Smiles signal approachability, happiness and confidence. Professional models have techniques to help them get in the mood and smile. Here's my favorite. Put your face about ten inches in front of a mirror. Look at yourself right in the eye and say the word "great" in as many different ways as you can: angry, loud, soft, sexy, keep going. Eventually you'll crack up. Repeat the exercise once a day for three days.

The next time you're on your way on stage say "great" under your breath three times and you'll be smiling.

Control your Breathing

Use a technique like Square Breathing (breathe in counting to four, hold for four, out for four, hold for four. Repeat ten times) to help you relax and overcome the fear of public speaking immediately before you go on stage.

Open your Body Language

Body language can be loosely broken into two kinds of signals, open or closed.

Open body language exposes your heart and is welcoming, while closed body language defends the heart and appears standoffish and sometimes aloof.

Open body language, together with open facial expressions, includes uncrossed arms and legs, ease in facing the audience, good eye contact, smiling, standing or sitting erect, flexible shoulders and a generally relaxed aura. Open body language makes expressive use of hands, arms, legs and feet.

Show Some Personality

Let your personality shine through in your presentation. It will allow you to better connect and communicate with your audience.

Don't Try Too Hard – Take it Easy

In a study conducted at Princeton University, students were questioned about their methods of analyzing people they met for the first time. Over-eagerness was one of the most reported turnoffs. Smile naturally, joke naturally and resist the temptation to be patronizing.

If you're putting on an act, you'll come across as a phony. Sure, be friendly and smile, but avoid having a grin on your face all the time. People who don't know when to stop grinning end up appearing insecure and foolish.

Conquering Last-Minute Butterflies and First-Minute Jitters

Move. Fortunately your mind and body are all part of the same system. You can't feel shy with your hands in your back pocket, you can't feel nervous while jumping in the air with your arms and legs spread wide apart. Just before you go on, find a private place (the bathroom will do) and shake your body out.

At-the-Podium Anxiety

Find a friendly face in the audience. They're always out there, the "Nodders." Bless them, they are nodding away, agreeing with you and smiling. They usually make up about 5 percent of the audience. Find three or four and keep coming back to them for comfort.

Blanking Out

Have a life-raft. Many speakers, especially those who don't use notes, occasionally blank out. It can be for many reasons: sometimes you get side-tracked, other time you do the same speech more than once in a day and can't remember if you said something already or not.

Always have a life-raft up your sleeve. In interactive speeches, stop and ask questions related to your topic, "Has anybody experienced…?", but they can be questions as simple as, "Does anybody have any questions so far?" Use this opportunity to glance at your notes.

StorySpeak Where Possible

Direct your audience to their senses. Talk about the way things look, sound and feel. It makes for a much richer presentation. Throw in i-Kolas from time to time. Repeat your point and squeeze in the title of your speech every ten minutes or so.

At first it might seem awkward and embarrassing to jump up in front of people you don't know, or don't know very well, and fire them up. But, with a little practice, it soon becomes second nature.

Infect the Audience with your Enthusiasm

Allow your passion and vision to command the audience's full attention.

Things to avoid.

Sloppy presentations. Crowded Slides. Making jokes at the audience's expense. Loosing your audience in jargon. Over-the-top shtick, "is everybody happy!!"

13
Practicing

The catch-22 of public speaking is that the more you do it, the easier it becomes. The problem is that most of us don't have much chance to gain that experience. Sure, naturally outgoing people are generally more comfortable than the more introspective types but there's no substitute for experience. And there are a lot of ways that you can get that experience.

When our children were young, my wife and I made a deal with them. On the first Tuesday of each month, at supper time, we would "visit" a foreign country. Our five children decided which country they wanted to visit each month, and Wendy and I would research the menu and prepare a typical three-course meal from the chosen destination.

During dinner each child agreed to give a two or three minute, informal presentation about predetermined aspects of the country, climate, tourism, industry, politics, exports.

We all had a month to prepare. I remember answering the phone on one occasion to be told, "This is the Mexican consulate, may I please speak to Sandy?" Sandy was ten at the time and had phoned asking for information. This was before the internet. The information subsequently arrived in the mail.

At first, the kids were shy and nervous, but before long

they were learning from one another how to research and make their talks enjoyable and informative. Guests would sometimes join us at the table and get in on the fun and we never took the content too seriously.

These entertaining adventures continued for more than a year, and we had a wonderful time. Today, as adults they don't think twice when they have to give a talk or a presentation.

Do you think this exercise helped them at school and later on in life? You bet. Do you think it's ever too early, or too late, to start learning a skill as valuable as this?

No. Find a way to practice your speaking skills. You can start small even by just telling folks over coffee about an interesting article you read in the paper or online.

Part Two:
Speak and get Paid

The overarching objective of any top-notch speech is the audience wants to be entertained and informed and receive tools they can use immediately. That means your speech must be liberally sprinkled with StorySpeak and really useful, practical, hands-on tips: invented or re-invented by you the speaker.

It's paramount that you know what unique benefits you can offer the audience that other speakers can't. A benefit in this context is anything that makes their lives more profitable, efficient, faster, cheaper, friendlier, happier, smarter, quieter, funnier—you name it.

You need to know who your audience is and why they will listen to you. So, ask yourself, "What does my audience want and how will they know when they've got it?"

Businesses and speaker bureaus are looking for speakers who offer a promise and deliver on it. If a corporation has a 'problem' they need help with, your speech must help solve the problem.

Businesses and speaker bureaus want your speech to give a fresh take. This can take many forms—a lively, irreverent voice and excellent stories; new expertise on a topic, new solutions; a unique new way of presenting material. For example, Convince Them in 90 Seconds or Less brings the time component to a much-covered topic."

If there's one area that aspiring professional speakers make or break it, it's in the trustworthiness department. If you want to become a successful speaker and get noticed, you need to start working on your credentials and your credibility at the same time as you start crafting your speech.

Credentials demonstrate your trustworthiness as an expert. They come in many forms: a document or certificate proving your professional qualification like an economist, professor or doctor might have. Maybe you have your own radio or TV show or you're a well respected entrepreneur, blogger, newscaster, author, sports personality, celebrity or record holder.

Your credibility comes from third-party endorsements, and the bigger the better. It doesn't mean much if your Uncle Oscar and the lady at Walgreens thinks you're fabulous. You need the guys at Business Television, the business bloggers or the president of Campbell's soup to say you're great.

If you want people to pay you to speak tomorrow you need start collecting, compiling and earning your credentials today.

14
Stepping-stones to a great speech or pitch

If a business story is kind of like a shish-kebab, a great speech is kind of like picking your way across a fast-flowing stream on stepping-stones and taking your audience along with you. The stream is the topic, and the stones are the steps to an outcome or solution. Five stones are usually sufficient to begin with. You open your speech on one bank, step onto the different stones on the way across the stream, and close your speech as you step onto the far bank.

At the start, standing at the river's edge, you set up your speech, state your point and get emotional buy-in from your audience.

Stepping onto the first stone you explain the goal, problem or dilemma. Moving out onto the second stone you explain what's coming up on the next few stones. For example, if you're pitching to Venture Capitalists your next three stepping-stone topics might be 1, your product, 2,

your team and 3, your marketing strategy. If you are motivating the board to embrace Artificial Intelligence in banking your stones might be 1, technical innovations, 2, consumer applications and 3, the future of AI. If you're rallying a sales team to bring in more business your stones might be 1, signs of dysfunction, 2, new targets and 3, staying focused.

CROSSING THE STREAM TO A BRIGHTER FUTURE

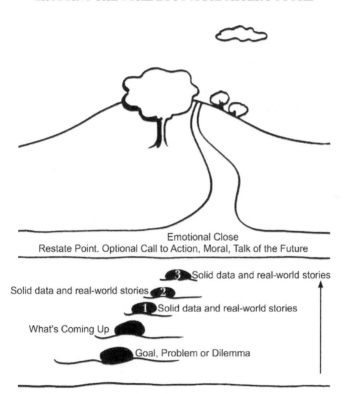

Emotional Close
Restate Point. Optional Call to Action, Moral, Talk of the Future

3 Solid data and real-world stories

Solid data and real-world stories 2

1 Solid data and real-world stories

What's Coming Up

Goal, Problem or Dilemma

Hook, Point and Emotional Opening to Get Audience Buy-in

Each of these stones will hold a selection of solid data and real-world stories; in other words, carefully prepared facts and figures and shish-kebabs.

As you step onto the far bank, you deliver your emotional close and restate your point. As you talk about the future, you can invite your listeners to imagine themselves in the same situation, and use what they learned from your speech to resolve the problem. Prompt your listeners to visualize how to apply what they've heard: "Just imagine . . . ," "Picture yourself in the future when . . . ," "The next time you are faced with . . ."

15
Hitting the pay-streak

Pay-Streak:
A vein of oil, gold, or any other
deposit that can lead to a fortune.

A t a few minutes to three the Escalade was parked on the far side of the Venetian bridge.

The smoked glass windows made it impossible to see if there was anyone inside so I went and stood where I could be easily seen. At three o'clock on the dot the driver's door opened and an elderly man in white overalls got out and marched in my direction. The bells in the Basilica chimed three times up above us and the man's face broke into a smile.

"Mister Nick?" he spoke softly with a trace of an accent.

I nodded.

"Mannie Esposito, I'm from Julia."

"Oh yes!" He picked up on my frown. I wasn't ready to smile back.

"She's waiting for me to bring you."

Beneath us I could hear the warbling notes of "O Sole Mio" as the Gondoliers serenaded their passengers.

A doorman passed and slapped the man on the shoulder, "Hey Mannie. Long time no see." My suspicion lessened a bit. At least he was known here.

"Thanks Paolito." The man nodded but his hound-dog eyes stayed focused on me.

"You know something?" he said leaning in way too close, "My wife is from Napoli. She share a secret with me. You hear that?" He paused and put his index finger to his right ear. "Gondoliers – in Italy they don't sing – they only sing in the movies. Ha! And even if they did, they'd a never sing "O Sole Mio because it's a Napoli song. That's like getting a Chicago lounge-singer to sing Swanee River. Ha!" He nodded his head and looked pleased with himself.

I hadn't noticed the yellow Motorola two-way radio in his hand until he lifted it to his mouth and squeezed it. "Hey Jules – I got him." He let go the talk button.

Her voice came through the tiny speaker. "Mister Boothman, this is Mannie. He's my," she paused, she was shouting and there was a flapping sound in the background, "he's my boss."

"What's going on Julia? Where are you?"

"I got a surprise for you. I'm only five minutes away. Please. Mannie will bring you."

It's just over a mile from The Venetian to The Circus Circus Hotel and Resort. Mannie spoke twice on the Motorola but I couldn't make out what he was saying. After a few minutes he turned left off the strip then north on

Sammy Davis Junior Drive and turned into the back of Circus Circus Adventuredome. We pulled in the parking lot at the exact moment a blue and white Robinson helicopter with SkyValley Tours painted on the side set down about a fifty feet to the right of the Escalade.

Mannie scooted around the limo and tugged my door open. Without speaking he waved me in the direction of the chopper. I didn't move. He cupped his hands and yelled "Go."

The passenger door on the chopper opened and a dark-haired woman in a purple skirt and white blouse got out and held on to the door. She waved at me to hurry. I could see a younger woman at the flight controls talking into a headset. Julia?

A crowd started to gather. The fascination with helicopters goes far beyond the people that fly in them. The mystique and romance they hold is the stuff of dreams - a symbol of wealth, power and authority.

"Go go go now." Said Mannie above the thwuping of the blades.

"Not a chance in hell!" I yelled back.

"Because she's a woman?"

"Hell no. Because I don't know any of you."

"You can know this. SkyValley is my company and that woman Julia, she's got more than two thousand hours flying helicopters."

Mannie put the Motorola to his mouth. "He's not going."

Julia looked over at me and raised her hands impatiently.

Mannie grabbed my shoulder and put his mouth close to

my ear. "Do what you feel is right. You got three seconds."

He looked away, waited, then spoke into the Motorola.

"Shut her down Jules," he said, "we change places." Then he turned to me. "She drive you back to the hotel in the limo so you can do your business there. Big pity. She had a very nice plan."

"Damn it." I should know better. "Ok. I'm going"

I ducked slightly and ran to the open door. The woman helped me in and closed it behind me. Julia snatched a headset from the passenger seat before I sat on it and thrust it at me.

"Where are you taking me?" I asked at the top of my voice.

"Belt." She yelled above the repeated thwuping of the blades and the flacking of the engine. I adjusted the four-way harness and fumbled the headset into place. The mechanical sounds faded into the background.

"McCarran Tower, helicopter Zero-Mike-Tango, request VFR departure out of Circus helipad to the east not above fifteen hundred, heading south leaving your area." It took me a moment to realize the voice in the headset really was Julia's.

I looked out my window and saw Mannie hugging the woman in the purple skirt. The Neopolitana I presume.

The reply came back fast. "Helicopter Zero-Mike-Tango, McCarran Tower, clear for takeoff, report one mile east at or below two thousand."

She confirmed the tower's instructions then jabbed me with her elbow and smiled. "Give me a minute."

With a smooth gentle touch she had us crabbing

sideways up and away from the helipad, over the Las Vegas Strip and east toward the Hoover Dam.

She was talking to the tower and methodically scanning the sky around us.

Fifteen minutes ago I was on the ground at The Venetian, now I'm a thousand feet in the air above it and halfway to the Hoover Dam.

She flicked us to intercom. "Give me a sec to get us out of here. Tower says there are over eighty aircraft in his control zone and I can only see four of them."

Shoot. I couldn't see any of them. No point protesting now. I decided to shut up and let her get on with it.

Two minutes later we turned right and headed south. Five minutes after that we set down in the parking lot across from what looked like a cowboy set from a wild west movie. The sign over the general store on the main street read Eldorado Canyon Mine.

I pulled off my headset.

"What the hell are we doing here?"

Julia ignored me until she finished her shut down procedure.

"Didn't expect this did you?" She said flicking three switches in quick succession. "You said finding your gift is like looking for a basket of gold right? What better place to look for gold than right here. This was the oldest, richest and most famous gold mine in Southern Nevada. Now it's a tourist trap."

With that, she pushed open her door, came around to my side and unlatched my side.

"I booked a space out back on the patio where we can

talk in private."

"Who's paying for this?" I said slapping the helicopter door.

"No-one." She said as she walked backwards in front of me and slung a red backpack over her left shoulder. "It's mine."

"On a limo driver's pay!"

Coolly she flexed her fingers, then she stopped. I nearly walked into her.

From my dad. You can spot more stray cattle in an hour in that than you can in a week on horseback.

"Big ranch?"

"Sixty-five thousand acres."

"Mannie ran the place. You don't mess with an ex-mercenary from Mozambique. He's hard as nails and utterly ruthless when he has to be. Kept my step-brothers in line; until my dad died."

We paused outside the general store. The half dozen tourists who'd rushed out to see the helicopter arrive drifted back to the store muttering about us.

"Wait here." She disappeared behind a mound of rusty cartwheels, tumbleweed and pumpkins, each one with a price tag attached, and into the store.

After the helicopter ride it was quiet here. Peaceful. I laughed.

Julia was back. "Come."

"Is that the end of the story?"

"Mannie taught me to fly when I was sixteen."

She led me around behind the store to a small barbecue area where a couple of homemade picnic tables and half a dozen homemade chairs, a redbrick outdoor fireplace with a chimney and an old-fashioned water tower like they have for filling up railroad engines, gave it the authentic historic look. Dark clouds sat atop the mountains in the background. I thought about the flash floods they had last weekend.

Julia dropped her knapsack on to one of the picnic tables.

"You okay with this?"

"Sure." I pulled a thesaurus out of my jacket pocket and put it on the table followed by a dozen or so folded blank sheets of paper from my inside pocket and a couple of pens. I looked again at the dark clouds. "We should get started."

We sat facing each other in the shade. It was utterly silent. Not a breath of wind. Julia marshaled her thoughts.

"'Find your pay-streak Julia.' Those were the last words my dad said to me." She screwed up her eyes and went silent for a moment. "He was an engineer turned prospector."

"Mining gold is easy," he'd say. "Finding the pay-streak, that's the problem. It can be right under your nose but you'll have no idea it's there for sure until you find it! You won't find it alone. You need a hound-dog to help you cause it's a real tricky trail." She gazed up at the black clouds on the mountains then turned to face me. "You call it a gift. He called it a pay-streak. I get it, either way."

I straightened out the sheets of paper absent-mindedly and neatly lined up the thesaurus and the pens. Then I took one of the sheets and folded it in half vertically.

"So, I'm your hound-dog? And you brought me this far so I wouldn't run away."

"Hound dogs are independent creatures and they don't stop until they find what they are looking for."

"Good, then close your eyes and relax," I said. "Looks like we've got some mining to do."

"Imagine in your mind's eye, that a few moments before you were born you found yourself in a lineup. In your hand you had a small piece of paper. On that piece of paper you had to write down why you deserve to be born. There's only one condition: it must be something to benefit humanity, a gift if you will, because we know we have evolution. Let's call that piece of paper your Statement of Fortune."

"Fortune is a beautiful word with many connotations: luck, future, fate, chance, destiny, affluence and blessed. At its essence though, fortune is an ongoing chain of unpredictable everyday miracles that turn out in your favor."

"When you get to the front of the lineup, they look at what you wrote and either say, 'that's not good enough get to the back and start again,' or else they say, 'that's great. You can be born now'."

"If that's the case, they send you over to the supply department to get outfitted for the trip. In the supply department, they look at your Statement of Fortune and say, 'okay, to share this Gift with the world you are going to need a unique combination of skills.' For example, some people skills, some organizational skills, a flair for languages, or whatever. They install a unique combination about 10 of these "core attributes" inside you - then off you go to get born."

"Unfortunately for you though, they tear up your Statement of Fortune and wipe your memory. So, here you find yourself, like everybody else, knowing you are uniquely equipped for something, but you don't know what it is. When you discover what was written on your Statement of Fortune your Gift will reveal itself."

"To find it we're going to work backwards and discover which attributes were placed inside you, but first you must accept the Cardinal Rule."

"Your Statement of Fortune is for your eyes, your head and your heart only. Reveal it before you live it, and it will evaporate before your eyes."

16
Revealing your Gift

Ask someone to give you ten words to describe themselves and you'll discover they can't. Not accurately. They might say they are "caring", "creative" or "organized" when, if you dig a little deeper, you discover that when they say caring, what they actually mean is "vigilant." They say "Creative" when what they really are is "inventive." And by "organized" they may really mean "methodical".

This may seem like splitting hairs but a caring, creative, organized person is not the same person as a vigilant, inventive, methodical person. If you are going to be a think-on-your-feet motivational speaker you have to know the real you and what comes naturally and what doesn't.

This becomes more obvious when you look at the negative words people use to describe themselves. I call them barrier-words. Words like "I am 'shy'," "I'm 'negative'," "I am 'anti-social'."

If someone believes these descriptions of themselves just imagine the catastrophic consequences of judgments made based on these beliefs. They are utterly inaccurate descriptions because shy, negative and anti-social are not core human strengths. Nobody was born that way.

Dig a little here and you might find "shy" becomes "cautious" or "reserved," "negative" becomes "competitive" and "anti-social" becomes "super social" Why?

Jackson told me he was shy. His mother told people he was shy when he was growing up. "Oh yes Jackson's such a shy boy." "Oh Jackson. Stop being so shy!" Well jeepers. He's listening too! And the seed is sown. When Jackson discovers there's no such thing as shy and he's actually "cautious and reserved", his negative self-esteem turns around in a flash and sends him down a different, stronger path.

After a speech I gave in St. Louis, Emilie said, "When you mentioned that bit about 'millions of introverts having to masquerade as extroverts just to make a living', you were so right. I planned this event tonight and I'm totally antisocial."

I told her I didn't believe there was such a thing. "I'm guessing," I said to her, "that you were probably born super-sociable. And when you were young someone hurt you so badly in your "super-sociableness" that you turned that particular "core attribute" upside down and said no-one is ever going to hurt me like that again. On the bottom of that attribute was written "anti social." But deep down you are still super-sociable"

"You are right." She hugged me with happy tears.

At a workshop Mehdi defined himself as negative. He explained, "I'll be in a meeting and someone comes up with a great idea and I get mad that I didn't come up with an idea like that myself." I pointed out that he was probably defining "competitive" not "negative". He was relieved to get closer to his true self.

These next three exercises work really well in pairs. If you can find someone you trust to do the exercise with you it's more fun and a lot easier. Just take turns with each exercise. For example person A says to person B, "give me 10 words to describe yourself." When person B gets stuck or runs out of things to say, "push" them. Say "and what else" and wait. Really dig deep. These three exercises normally take a couple of hours with two people. They are valuable even if you're not going to be a speaker.

Exercise 20: Ten Words

Write down ten words to describe yourself. Make sure they are the first words that your imagination throws at you. Make sure you write them down unedited. They can be good traits or bad traits. Chances are, after 5 words you'll say that's it, I don't have any more. But stay at it until you have all ten then take a break.

Exercise 21: What Do I Really Mean

Take each word your imagination threw at you and answer the question, "what do I really mean by (word number one)." Do this for all of the words then take another break.

Exercise 22: Defining Myself Accurately

Using a Roget's Dictionary Thesaurus, look up each of

the ten words you used to describe yourself and, referring to the notes you made in the last exercise, see if there's a better, more precise, more accurate word to replace your original word. Go through your list. Take your time.

Ben's Story

At fifty-six, Ben found his Unique Gift during one of my workshops. He surprised everyone when, not long afterwards, he gave up his career as an investment banker, raised three hundred thousand dollars through grants and sponsors and opened an authentic traditional bakery. The bakery was staffed, almost exclusively, by more than forty people in their early twenties who'd been in trouble with the law. Ben turned up one day unexpectedly at the beginning of a new class and asked to address the group. Here's what he said.

"The reason I drove all this way today was to share with you something that I did wrong when I took this workshop with Nick two years ago. I resisted. When I got the words right, after spending hours asking questions and writing out pages and pages to end up with such an obvious phrase, I actually said out loud to the whole group, 'You mean to say I actually paid money and drove all this way to end up with something so trite and simple. I expected more than this: it can't be right.' But I've come to tell you it was right. It was simple, so simple I couldn't believe it. Nick told us all it could take up to three months for what we'd done that day to fully click, to go right into our systems and affect us, and for us to get it. I left feeling cheated. But, less than two weeks later I woke up one morning and found I was crying. I crept into the bathroom and looked in the mirror at this guy who was me, and this voice from inside me just kept whispering, 'Oh my God, oh my God, oh my God.' And I got it! I was crying with happiness and I couldn't even put into words what I'd got."

Everyone in the room was staring at Ben. He continued. "It will be simple, it will be obvious, it is powerful and it will set you free. I also came here to warn you that if you tell your words to anyone else outside of this room before you "get it," before they dawn on you, you'll dilute the power and they will seem nothing and trivial. They are words that belong inside you, inside your mind, not outside and spoken, they are trivial outside you. When you know your Gift it will be your secret source of power that can guide and inspire you for the rest of your life, in all the decisions you make, not just in your work but on all levels of your life: your direction, your relationships and where you are going to live. It will be your sorcerer's stone. Once you get it, everything falls into place in ways that even Nick's metaphors can't explain. Everyday miracles happen before your eyes - things just fall into place. In the beginning you notice them. After a while they just become part of your unfolding, part of how you help the world go around." He seemed to come out of a trance. Ben looked around and smiled.

"The four words that changed my life, 'I shepherd lost sheep.' I feel comfortable sharing them with you here today because I am living my Gift. It is my purpose, my project and my passion."

These are the very same exercises that Ben did. And the same ones I spent four hours helping Julia with one late, muggy afternoon seven years ago at The Eldorado Canyon Mine near Las Vegas, Nevada.

No-One was Born a Bitch

Julia described herself, among other things, as an aggressive, angry bitch. Words she'd heard from her step-brothers growing up.

By the time she accurately reframed her strengths, aggressive shifted to resolute, angry to swift and bitchy to high standards. She realized how the people in her environment had flipped her strengths upside down.

Here are more examples with the perfect verb in capitals:

I SEARCH OUT and bring art to the world – Ralph Lauren

I CHALLENGE the status quo in everything I do – Steve Jobs

I MAKE learning fun – Brain Quest founder

We SPREAD understanding through stories – TED Talks founder

I GIVE women the courage to succeed - TalentedWomen founder

I SHEPHERD lost sheep - Ben

I CHALLENGE people to imagine wild, new ideas - Julia

Uncovering Your Statement Of Fortune

Do you remember Francesca's i-kola back on page 60

"I'm kind of like a Pit Bull because I'm watchful, loyal, and protective."

I spent another hour with Francesca and unearthed her

Gift. We extended her i-Kola, defined her accurately, played around with her loves, hates, enthusiasms etc., found her "perfect verb" (GUARD) and came up with: I guard against complacency.

Saying what makes her angry deep down was the tipping point.

"I hate it when people say, 'there's nothing we can do about it.' Because there's always lots we can do about it."

With some people, like Francesca, it's easy to spot when you finally get every word in place. There's a massive sense of relief and relaxation. With others, like Ben, there's so much resistance to the simplicity that it takes a little time. A bit like love at first sight. Emotional people get it immediately. Rational people take time. But the seed is sown.

Now that you have an accurate handle on how to understand the attributes inside you, let's try your own i-kola one more time. Go with your gut. Let an image bubble up.

I am kind of like a...

Because...

Let your gut guide you. Listen to your subconscious. Catching the first thing that comes to mind may well prove valuable. No matter how crazy the words seem, write them down.

Divide a legal-sized sheet of paper into four vertical columns. Label them one through four. Fold the sheet in half lengthways so you now have two columns on each side. The reason you're dong this is to find fresh connections between the columns and the words later when you unfold the sheet.

Keeping the sheet folded, write down in column #1 the 10 accurate words you use to describe yourself.

Exercise 23: Locate your Enthusiasms

Enthusiasm comes from the Latin word enthusiasmus, which roughly translates to "Divine Inspiration" or "God flowing through".

On a separate pad, write down 6 activities you enjoy doing where energy and time flow through you. They will be activities you do well and always have since you were young.

Refine and prioritize your list to three and add them to column #1 of your folded sheet.

Example of enthusiasms: seeing beauty in people, improvising solutions, playing with language

Exercise 24: Finding Your Perfect Verb

Look for the verbs behind your Enthusiasms. Determine what actions are required to do these activities. Look for action verbs like challenge, analyze, connect, create, simplify, promote, present, organize, rather than abstract verbs like caring, helping and showing.

Refine and prioritize your list to three and, keeping the sheet folded, turn it over and write them in column #4.

Examples of verbs behind them: I revere, I release, I simplify

Exercise 25: Finding Your Natural talents

List your natural talents (things you were born with and come effortlessly - a talent for art, cooking, teaching, managing, seeing options, peacemaking). List the things that come naturally, effortlessly and easily to you. Look especially for those natural talents you perhaps take for granted. Maybe people have told you "You have a fantastic memory." "You never give up when you want something." "You can make people comfortable." "You seem to see beyond what people are saying." "You bring out the best in others." "You can sum things up in a flash."

Refine and prioritize your list to three and write them in column #4 of your folded sheet.

Examples of natural talents: seeing beyond people, a Gift for metaphor, persuasive

Exercise 26: Finding Your Attributes

Look for the Attributes (patience, curiosity, empathy, enthusiastic, courage, imaginative, humor, organizational skills, eloquence, etc.) behind your talents. Describe them only in the positive.

Refine and prioritize to three and write add them to column #4.

Examples of attributes behind talents: curiosity, enthusiasm, imagination

Exercise 27: What Makes You Excited or Happy?

In column #2 list three moral standards that give you joy deep down. (not fish and chips or the latest Corvette).

Moral standards that effect humanity.

Examples of moral standards that give you deep joy: decency, dignity, the power of focused minds,

Exercise 28: What Makes You Angry or Extremely Sad?

In column #4 list three moral standards that make you angry or extremely sad deep down.

Examples of moral standards that make you angry or extremely sad: wasted human potential, lack of physical awareness, rudeness

Exercise 29: Who Will Benefit from your Gift

Outside of your family and friends, who in the world do you care about most? Which segments of society deserve to benefit from your Gift?

List seven and prioritize to three.

Unfold your sheet of paper and put them in column #2.

Putting It All Together

Chose one characteristic from each of these pairs and write them in column #3.

Big-picture or Details

I simplify or I complicate

More rational or More emotional

Controller or Analyst

Supporter or Entertainer

Exercise 30: My i-Kola

From the list below, circle all the personalities that resonate with your character as being true of you. They are not literal. For example you might not be an architect but you might feel you are kind of like an architect in how you structure teams or configure your social life. Add the words to column #3. Feel free to include any of your own words too.

entertainer, adversary, commander, architect, guardian, beacon, composer, biographer, brigand, matchmaker, servant, wayfarer, map-maker, reviewer, organizer, challenger, champion, prospector, counselor, clown, wrangler, cheerleader, companion, ambassador, constructor, explorer, inventor, mechanic, ranger mercenary, messenger, adventurer, navigator, performer, rebel, scavenger, supporter, watcher, shepherd – add to the list if you wish.

Before you go any further unfold your worksheet and make five photocopies of it and fold them all. Like this, you have an original and five spares in case you want to start over.

On a fresh sheet of paper write out the following in large letters:

I am kind of like a _____

I_____

do_____

for_____

so they can _____

Make five photocopies of this sheet too.

This pattern is only a guide to get you started. Once you have this filled in you'll want to massage your statement into something simpler. Remember, your Statement of

Fortune is for your eyes, your mind and your heart only.

Now you are ready to look for connections and create the first draft of your Statement of Fortune. Find somewhere comfortable, where you won't be disturbed. Perhaps at a friendly café. It's inspiring to see people as you work at it. They are, after all, the reason for your endeavors.

Exercise 31: Create your Statement of Fortune

The architecture of a Statement of Fortune looks like this:

"I am kind of like a (insert your i-Kola) because I (insert your perfect verb) (insert what you do) for (insert the intended beneficiary) in order that they can (insert benefit).

Begin by taking something that excites you and use it to benefit something that angers or massively saddens you. Use your natural talents and flairs to fill in the gaps.

How your subconscious works with you

Have you ever been reading a magazine or newspaper and suddenly you flip back automatically and find something you've been looking for? That's your subconscious right there. It knew you were looking for this and saw you'd missed it so it signaled to you, "Go back two pages, top left, you're looking for that."

Finding your "perfect verb" is the first milestone. You'll find it lurking somewhere just below the surface of your talents. As you stare at the list, something beckons you.

Something is taking shape, something feels good in your body, and it feels right. Let your subconscious help you.

From your notes find a group of people that you care about or are drawn to: your intended beneficiary. The more specific the group the better. In Ben's case for example he had the metaphor "lost sheep," as one of his intended beneficiaries.

Armed with your perfect verb and a good idea of your beneficiary glance around your notes for words that jump out at you and those that just don't feel right. Your subconscious is watching all this and will give you a sense of what is right, even if it's something you want to consciously dismiss.

Aim for as few words as possible: four to eight is enough. "I make learning fun." "I connect people and ideas." "I give women the courage to succeed." "I challenge people to imagine wild, new ideas." "I illuminate choices." "I shepherd lost sheep." "I make complicated concepts sound simple and interesting."

These simple phrases all changed lives dramatically.

You will absolutely know when you are getting close. You will feel it. It will be obvious. Some people offer resistance at this point because they think it's too obvious - but it wasn't obvious before.

The simpler the Statement the better. When you watch someone go through this process you can tell by their face as they get close.

It relaxes and they light up inside. Many report it's like

floating. It's best summed up in this email after one of my seminars. "I woke up this morning and felt like I'd lost forty pounds."

Exercise 32: Edit your Statement of Fortune

You will edit and alter this many times over the coming days. Like Ben's example: "I shepherd lost sheep."

At this stage, while referring back to your previous notes you can alter anything you wish. Read through what you have written, circle anything that stands out. You will have the beginnings of your Statement of Fortune. Your subconscious will start churning and send you intuitions.

It may take hours or even months before you accept what you have in your draft statement. At first you may think "it can't be this it's too simple, it's too obvious." Disregard that thought. When it does come it will be obvious and it will be simple. Most great thoughts and ideas are obvious and simple. Every word must fit. If even one word feels wrong, take your statement apart and come at it again.

———————

By nine-fifteen I'd finished helping Julia. Tears of despair had turned to tears of joy. The sky was clear and so was Julia's Statement of Fortune. I scooped up the coffee cups and pizza plates we'd gone through in the last five hours. Julia pulled a portable Garmin GPS and a notepad out of her knapsack. She rhymed off wind velocity, atmospheric pressure, gyro settings and made notes on a small pad.

"Everything looks alright for the flight," she said, "but me, I'm exhausted." She stood up and took a phone out of the front pocket. "I'm going to find a signal and get hold of Mannie. He'll meet us and take you back."

The next morning Julia drove me to the airport. "Thank you." She said quietly as she handed me my carry-on. "I think I know what to do next"

So did I. I quietly slipped the envelope with the thousand dollars onto the front seat.

"What's this?" she asked.

"I told you I couldn't take it."

Three years later I was giving a keynote speech in Portland, Oregon. Walking through the convention center someone called out to me. Same red hair, more stylish now, same bright blue eyes, same Patek Philippe: same crocodile strap. She was speaking at a corporate event that day for the Department of Agriculture and was scheduled to speak at the Million Dollar Round Table in a couple of months. Julia was well on her way to being a top-flight speaker. Julia's Gift: I challenge people to imagine wild new ideas. Julia's speech? "Vital Risks – Vital Rewards".

Armed with her Gift and her StorySpeak raconteur style, Julia was transformed and energized. And her lucky breaks just kept on coming.

17
So, you want to be a motivational speaker?

Motivation and inspiration are rare commodities in today's society. As more and more people feel their lives lack purpose, direction and depth, their work lacks vitality and becomes mechanical. Talents are wasted, spirits are crushed and they feel lonely. So they seek motivation. This is where you come in. Because you, if you really desperately and passionately want to, can provide motivation and inspiration.

Motivation by it's very definition is temporary: the word actually means to provide someone with an external motive or a reward, or a bribe to do something. Inspiration by it's definition is permanent because it comes from the inside.

There's no shortage of books and courses in the marketplace that teach presentation skills, public speaking skills and even how to become a motivational speaker. You may have tried one or two. Some are very good. But most of them tack skills on to you from the outside. Stand like this, hold your hands like that, tell them what you're going to tell them, tell them, tell them what you told them - start like this, finish like that.

Don Jenkins, Vice President of National Speakers Bureau in Chicago, cautions "beware of tired and confusing advice about how you should stand, move, breathe, dress and patronize your audience. Some of the best speakers I've ever seen have lousy technique but their passion for their topic is infectious and captivating."

Derek Sweeney of The Sweeney Agency points out, "if you're being paid ten thousand dollars to speak for an hour, that's one hundred and sixty-seven dollars a minute. Don't waste your client's money on saying thank-you to all kinds of people and telling them how wonderful it is to be here today, get on and start delivering the goods."

The StorySpeak system echo's Don's and Derek's approach. It digs down inside you a little way to reveal two natural skills:

a gift for championing something you care desperately about

your natural potential to be a raconteur - someone who can make even mundane things sound interesting and amusing

Blend these two natural-born human attributes together with a hook, a point, some steak, some sizzle, a fresh take and a dose of stagecraft and you are well on your way to becoming a professional, motivational speaker.

It's not enough to have great knowledge or a strong message you need a charismatic style to go with it. At a recent debrief, put together by a the nation's #1 data network after a two day event with twelve speakers, audience members were asked to give feedback face-to-face.

"Just because someone is smart or has done something

amazing doesn't mean they belong on a stage," Janelle told the panel. "Just try sitting through ninety minutes of a really smart person who sucks on stage. You may as well poke your eyes out."

"Great speakers make time fly." Said Arpita, "Boring speakers are agony."

"I enjoy these sessions and they make me feel good," said Martin. "But do the speakers really motivate me? Most of them, no. Maybe for a day or two I feel full of energy and motivated. However my life was normal from the next day or the day after. But two of the speakers," big ear to ear grin, "oh definitely."

"The better the ability of the motivator," McKenzie, the organizer, told the panel, "the bigger the effect on the people being motivated, that is why we pay them. We need, and will continue to need, people who can actually deliver the goods and not just promises."

Alan Stevens, past President of The Global Speakers Federation maintains, "If motivational speakers don't make a difference they shouldn't get paid."

The aim of any speaker should be to leave a lasting impact, long after they have spoken. If they fail to do that, they are not truly professional. The best speakers, of any type, know how to provide lasting value.

By now, you're on the way to finding your gift and are starting to talk and think with a raconteur's style. You are familiar with hooks, points, steak and sizzle. And you have created opportunities to practice your Stagecraft.

A Motivational Speech has:

- a "killer title" with
- a unique benefit for
- a definable market
- A Motivational Speaker is:
- credible
- passionate
- media friendly and
- proves a single point with steps and stories

Once you have a topic in mind, one that fits with your Gift, then the sooner you can answer these 8 questions the closer you are to speaking and getting paid.

As a motivational speaker:

What's my killer/working title?

What's my speech all about?

Who, specifically, is my speech aimed at?

Why do they HAVE TO learn what I have to offer?

What's the unique benefit I offer my audience?

What's my fresh take?

Who the heck am I?

"When you've finished listening to my speech you'll be able to…"

Question number eight is "the ultimate question." It is the payoff, the benefit, the reward. It gives your speech "legs." In other words it gets passed along from person to person.

Exercise 33: A letter to a friend of a friend

Here's an exercise to breath life into your speech idea.

Write a three-part letter to a friend of a friend (someone who doesn't know you directly) telling them all about your speech.

Take as long as you need to outline the three parts.

The first part must include:

A statistic about your topic

The point of your speech

Some impressive information about who you are and why the person should trust you

Why you are moved to give this speech

Why your speech is different from all the others

The second part must include:

Who, specifically, is your ideal audience member

A brief, true story, relevant to why you are giving this motivational speech

What is the unique benefit to the listener

Why the listener would want to hear your message

The third part must include:

What you are going to be talking about

What's your promise to your listener

How are you going to keep your promise

Another brief, true story relevant to your topic

Finesse your words into a 5 minute speech. Make your words warm and friendly and speak in a voice any eight-year-old child could understand.

Practice saying it until you can do it in your sleep.

Exercise 34: Due Diligence

Who is the biggest expert in the world, the country and my community on your particular topic, and why?

a) World

b) Country

c) Community

Exercise 35: Benefits

What is my fresh take?

Why is my speech better than the other experts?

Who, specifically, will benefit from my speech?

What do I want to speak about and why?

What knowledge and experience do I have on this subject?

What is the unique benefit to audience members and why?

Exercise 36: Polishing your speech

Write out your speech in full and transfer it to your teleprompter program, either on your desktop or your laptop. It is too difficult to see it on your smart phone, and carrying it around with you in your hand and looking at it completely spoils your delivery.

Once you have perfected the elements of your speech you can transfer them to your smartphone to use as a reminder later.

Practice delivering your speech standing up and moving around. Restate your point from time to time.

18
Your official introduction

There are those "expert speaking coaches" who will tell you that you need to establish early on to your audience why they should listen to what you have to say. They'll tell you to highlight your background and expertise upfront and tell a personal story that reveals something about you or your experience to create a connection.

This is fine for most speakers but it's a big bucket of cold water to a motivational speaker. A motivational speaker hits the ground running.

The first impression the audience is going to gets of you will come from your official introduction, the person who is delivering it and the way they say it. This is why I started off Part Two by encouraging you to work on your Creds and Credibility. You need them now.

Below is a copy of my official introduction as an example because it fits a pretty standard pattern. It was passed on to me by a very successful speaker.

After it you will find a fill-in-the-blanks version to start working on your own introduction. You must, as I did, update it every time you have something more impressive to add.

Our speaker today has been called "one of the leading experts in face-to-face communication <u>in the world</u>" by The New York Times.

He has taught his revolutionary techniques of "Risk, and Rapport by Design" to thousands of corporations, colleges and universities around the world including the <u>Harvard and London Business schools</u>.

His first two books, How to Make People Like You in 90 Seconds <u>or Less</u> and How to Connect in Business in 90 Seconds <u>or Less</u> have sold more than 3 million copies and been translated into more than 30 languages.

A former fashion and advertising photographer who dealt with hundreds of new faces a week for clients like AT&T, Revlon and Coca-Cola, he is now recognized as a world-renowned expert in <u>turning first impressions into profitable relationships</u>.

The New York Times calls him "the new Dale Carnegie," the Economist Magazine calls him "truly inspirational," and Good Morning America says, "His book is my bible!"

Ladies and Gentlemen, please welcome ....Nicholas Boothman.

Now it's your turn.

Exercise 37: Your official introduction

Our speaker today has been called "_____"
by _____.

He/she has taught his/her revolutionary techniques of
"_____" to _____ including
_____.

His/her (credentials go here)

_____

_____

_____

_____

He/she is an expert in

_____

_____

_____ calls him/her "_____"

_____ calls him/her "_____"

_____ calls him/her "_____"

Ladies and Gentlemen, please welcome ....
_____.

My introduction is always accompanied by a note to the
person introducing me:

A SPECIAL NOTE TO NICHOLAS' INTRODUCER

Your role as an introducer is important.

The first impression the audience gets of me, comes from

you.

Research has shown that a properly prepared and presented introduction has a very large effect on how well a speaker is received by the audience.

Here are a few tips that "introducers" have found to be helpful …

1. Please practice reading this introduction a few times <u>before</u> delivering it to your audience.

2. Get in the mood, then deliver it to your audience with energy and enthusiasm!

3. Take your time – pause for moment after each paragraph.

I look forward to meeting you at the Conference prior to my presentation!

Kindest Regards

One final tip. Never, ever, let a client put together their own introduction for you from bits and pieces picked-up off the internet. Sure, if they know you well, they can adlib around your supplied official intro, but it is vital that the third-party credentials in your intro are read out and heard by the audience.

19
Attracting clients

For many years I made a very good living as a photographer in the fashion business. In June 1994, I was invited to speak about my work at the North York Camera Club in Toronto.

"How can I make this interesting?" I wondered. "I know I'll talk for five minutes about photography and fifty-five minutes about connecting with people. After all, that's what a fashion photographer does all day long."

When I'd finished my talk, three people came up to me: a doctor, a teacher and someone who trained airline personnel. "Can you come and give this talk to my people?" they each asked. "Not the photography bit, the rest. The connecting with people part."

That night I told my wife Wendy, "I've got a new job. No more jet lag and moody models, no more gossiping hair dressers and yawning assistants, and no more finding myself on a beach at five in the morning in the pouring rain waiting for the sun to appear! I'm going to be a speaker."

When I woke up the next morning, Wendy asked me, "Still want to be a speaker?"

"Yes, I do."

"So, now what?" she asked.

"I'm not sure yet."

"Why not treat organizing a speaking engagement as if it were a photo shoot?" She replied. "If you were hired to do a shoot of a speaker with an audience, what would you do?"

"Simple. I'd book some space at a local hotel and invite a bunch of people to come and listen."

"Well, what are you waiting for?"

By noon that day, I'd rented half of the ballroom at our local Holiday Inn for a date two weeks from then and invited a bunch of friends, clients, models and suppliers to come and hear me talk about "Rapport by Design," which is the working title I came up with for my approach to connecting with people.

"Twenty-nine bucks a head," I told them, "and bring your friends." Eighty people showed up. I was buzzed. The event was a success.

I started talking to anyone who'd listen, Rotary Clubs, associations, networking groups, but my progress up the speaking ladder was slow. A model I knew had a contact at a hot TV show in Toronto called *Breakfast Television*. I wangled my way on.

It was March, so I talked to kids looking for summer jobs about the value of people skills. I offered to go to any school and talk to job-seeking students about interviewing skills, for free. By the end of the day, nine schools had agreed to have me come, and in only a month, I spoke to fourteen hundred kids.

But my new speaking career was still moving too slowly for me, and because I'd pushed my photography aside, my income was taking a nosedive. What was missing? I reviewed my resources, and it hit me like a champagne cork. A book! And preferably a best seller with a killer title.

I traded in my cameras for a laptop and started to write but I didn't have a clue where to start. Then a couple of things happened that changed everything.

The editor of our village newspaper stopped me outside the bakery and said she'd seen me on *Breakfast Television*. "Why don't you write an article for the paper about making people like you?" she asked.

Why not? I figured an article might even form the basis of a chapter for my book. The first article came so easily, I wrote a second. Both later became chapters.

The following week, a friend invited me to speak about "Rapport by Design" at an environmental fair she was promoting. In the afternoon, my friend told me she'd convinced the guy from the nightly news to talk to me about my book.

I was excited to see him and his cameraman approach. He came right up and said, "I hear you're writing a book."

"Yes," I said proudly.

"So, what's it called?"

"It's about rapport by design."

"Oh," he said and all the energy drained from his face. "And what's it about?"

"How to make people like you in about ninety seconds," I chirped out of nowhere.

"Nice," he said and the energy returned.

Then I added with a flourish, "Or less!"

"Love it. Got it," he said. "What's the point of your book?"

"When people like you, they see the best in you and they

look for opportunities to say 'yes' to you. And, they make that decision in the first few seconds of seeing you."

"How am I doing then?" he said, flirting with the camera.

"Oh, yes," I said. "I like you already."

"Well, there you have it, folks! How to make people like you in ninety seconds."

"*How to Make People Like You in 90 Seconds or Less*," I chimed back.

"When is it coming out?" he asked.

"Soon." I said.

Perfect! I'd found my killer title.

My beliefs were confirmed three days later when I got a call from the acquisitions editor of a well-known Canadian publishing house. Their president had seen me on TV and was offering to buy the world rights for *How to Make People Like You in 90 Seconds or Less*.

"But I haven't written it yet." I said.

"Don't worry about that," the publisher said. "We'll take care of it!"

It was tempting because I was running out of money fast, but I thanked him and turned down his offer. But I had learned a valuable lesson about the power of a killer title in the motivation world.

Energized, I wrote with a vengeance for the next three weeks. Then I got a call to speak at a Substitute Teachers' conference. They too had seen me on *Breakfast Television*. "Bring copies of your book," they urged.

"That's it. Enough writing." I cleaned up my manuscript and got a local printer to run off two-hundred copies.

We sold every copy except for the fifteen copies I slipped

into my briefcase.

The next day, I mailed fourteen of them to different literary agents in the States and put the remaining copy in my desk.

Ten days later, I got a call from an agent who had sold How to Make people Like You in 90 Seconds or Less to a New York publishing house and got me a six figure advance. That little book made my speaking career explode.

Moral of the story? Package your expertise and gain instant credibility.

A well-written self-help book by a media-friendly author can substantially increase your speaking fees and bookings. It is kind of like a magic wand and a bunch of ambassadors rolled into one and working for you twenty-four hours a day.

Your book can sell your expertise, build your brand and do your PR work, even while you're sleeping. It's your calling card, a demonstration of your worth and part of your legacy. Its potential to open doors is almost unlimited.

20
A happy ending

It was 2:15 in the morning when I got to the front of the lost baggage line at O. R. Tambo International Airport in Johannesburg, South Africa. The flight was delayed twelve hours in London and somewhere along the way British Airways managed to make my checked bags disappear – as it turned out later - forever.

I filled in the lost-luggage forms while Robert, the event planner and two assistants waited for me outside the baggage claim area. I'd called him to let him know I was tied-up.

At last, hanging on to my trusty shoulder bag, I emerged apologetic.

"Don't worry," said Robert, "It's just great to know you're here. This is Kayla."

A silver-haired woman in a blue gingham shirt and tight white pants with a wide brown belt stroked her magnificent ponytail and leaned forward.

"I've watched your presentations online. I'm very happy to meet you in person."

I felt as if my feet had just touched solid ground for the first time since I left my farm in Canada two and a half days earlier.

"Thanks," I said. "I guess I'll have to go shopping for a suit, shirt, shoes and all that in the morning."

"It'll be okay. We'll help you." Robert said. "I know the exact spot - not three minutes from the hotel."

A lanky young man in long grey shorts and a Blue Jays jersey approached smiling, carrying a plastic tray. He put out his right hand and made eye-contact while balancing the tray with the other hand. "Hi. I'm Denis." His handshake was as friendly as his smile.

"Nice shirt." I said.

"Been quite the night," Robert said as he reached onto the tray and handed me a coffee and a bundle of warm foil. "We're still waiting for one more speaker to clear customs. Coming in from Sydney, Australia."

Robert held the coffee while I peeled back the foil to reveal a steaming roast beef sandwich.

"She's been flying all night. One of the busiest women on the speaking circuit."

"I know." I said. "I read the program."

I bit into the sandwich and sipped the hot coffee.

"Why not go with Kayla and get settled in the car. Shouldn't be much longer."

"Just what I need." I raised the cup and the sandwich. "Thanks."

By the time we reached the car the sandwich and the coffee were gone. Kayla took the packaging and held open the rear passenger-side door of the stretch Mercedes.

Alone in the back I thought, 'Robert knows where I'm going. This is where I go to sleep.' I shut my eyes and winced at the thought of replacing everything in a few hours. The next flight carrying my bags wouldn't arrive until after my speech and there was no way I could go on stage in front of fifteen hundred financial planners at the Nelson Mandela Convention Center in the same jeans, Blundstones, blue denim shirt and tweed jacket I'd been wearing for the trip.

I don't know how long I napped but when I came around I was sprawled across the back seat. I opened my eyes. Robert was at the wheel. I sat up. We were cruising along an empty expressway between brightly lit office towers in downtown Johannesburg. It took me a moment to get my bearings.

The person in front of me was leaning against a huge white bed pillow jammed between her head and the window. She must have heard me stir.

"I thought you don't do red-eyes Nick."

I smiled to myself and leaned forward.

"I see you appreciate a real pillow Julia."

"Yes. And looks like I'm still sitting in the front of the car."

About the author

Nicholas Boothman is 'Dale Carnegie for a rushed era" according to the New York Times. The Economist Magazine calls him 'truly inspirational,' and Good Morning America says, 'His book is my bible.'

British by birth, Canadian by choice and Universal in his message, Nicholas has taught his revolutionary techniques of StorySpeak and Rapport by Design to thousands of corporations, colleges and universities around the world including the Harvard and London Business schools.

In 1982, he founded the advertising company Corporate Images and created powerful corporate presentations for almost every well-known company in North America.

Later, he founded Persuasion Technology Group and spoke at "Leadership from the Ground Up," along with Tom Peters, Ted Turner, Richard Branson, Stephen Covey and Ken Blanchard.

More than 600 corporations, thousands of small businesses, and six of the world's leading business schools have contacted him to rally and inspire their staff to take risks, connect, communicate and articulate their business ideas.

www.nicholasboothman.com

Made in United States
North Haven, CT
19 February 2024

48916197R00088